THINGS I DIDN'T LEARN IN BIBLE SCHOOL

THINGS I DIDN'T LEARN IN BIBLE SCHOOL

DR. C. M. WARD

WITH JEFFREY PARK

Foreword by Jim Bakker

BRIDGE PUBLISHING, INC.

Publishers of

LOGOS • HAVEN • OPEN SCROLL

Foreword

Once on the "PTL Club," Dr. C.M. Ward looked sternly into the camera and said, "If you have lost your sense of humor—you have stayed too long. You do not need revival, you are ready for formaldehyde!"

Dr. Ward has never been accused of losing his sense of humor, I'm sure. And all you have to do to prove that point is to read just a few paragraphs—any few paragraphs—of this delightful book.

It's the kind of book you pick up and don't want to put down until you've read every word. It's filled with the kind of tales that preachers are famous for swapping over dinner—sort of the "a funny thing happened to me on the way to church" kind of tales.

But the difference is, all of this is pure C.M. They are all his stories. It's funny. It's inspiring. It's full of the Word of God. It preaches a message without preaching. And that's a lot like C.M. himself.

I consider C.M. nothing short of a legend. For over a quarter of a century, he served as radio evangelist for "Revivaltime," the international voice of the Assemblies of God. Over 650 stations broadcasted his program to faithful listeners each week.

But C.M. is more than a great man of God whom I admire. He is a close and very dear friend to me. Before

PTL was so well known, C.M. came to our little studio and befriended Tammy and me. Over the years, as we have faced different crises, C.M. has always offered gentle words of encouragement and love. I'll never forget him for that.

I've often said that C.M. is my favorite preacher. And he really is. He is everything a preacher ought to be, plus he is a delight to listen to. I doubt that he has ever preached a boring sermon in all his life!

And the same can be said of the books he writes—especially this one! So sit back and enjoy, *Things I Didn't Learn in Bible School.* I know you'll enjoy it!

In warmest Christian love,
Jim Bakker

Contents

THINGS I
DIDN'T LEARN
IN BIBLE
SCHOOL

1

My First Pastorate

It smelled like a gas attack. But it was only Piggy Green coming to warm herself by the old-fashioned, pot-bellied stove.

Outside, the temperature was sub-zero. The little room in the church basement was the only one with a stove, so our little band of about a dozen parishioners and I carried on our Sunday morning services, trying hard not to breathe through our noses.

Actually, Piggy Green wasn't her real name. The people of the little Canadian community of Woodstock had fondly given her this nickname because of her peculiar habits.

Piggy had a green thumb. Everything she touched would grow. But she was also allergic to baths and when the heat would touch Piggy in our little subterranean sanctuary, the odor became horrendous.

Trying to preach without smelling was something I never learned in Bible school. In fact, quite a few experiences occurred during this first winter out of Central Bible Institute in Springfield, Missouri, for which I was not well prepared.

Like most any other new Bible school graduate, I was ready to take the world by the tail. My father was a well-known preacher in Pentecostal circles and especially in the Assemblies of God denomination, so I had something of an advantage over many of my classmates. Still there were no openings for a young whippersnapper preacher in our fledgling denomination back in 1928.

Finally, my dad took me to the city of my birth—Toronto, Canada, where he was to be the headliner at a very large convention. At the last service, before he read his text, he made a short announcement: "I have a boy here who has just graduated from Central Bible Institute. Is there anyone out there who can use him?"

Dad then read his text and preached brilliantly. I anxiously awaited the close of the service to meet the stampede of interested pastors. The service ended and I stood and waited and waited. No one came.

It was bad enough to be called "boy" by your dad. But to find that nobody—just nobody—wanted me, left me feeling hopeless and forsaken, with no money and no opening.

Finally, I started to leave when a man stopped me in the aisle. He said, "My name is Mr. Cole, I'm the auditor for the Marriott Marble Company in Montreal, and I feel God's been urging me to open a mission church in a section called Verdun. Maybe you can help."

Dad answered for me, "Yes, I believe he can." And in his bishop-like way (from his Methodist upbringing), Dad laid hands on me, prayed a short prayer and said, "Son, go with that man." To provide my "stake," Dad pulled a five-dollar bill from his pocket and gave it to me.

That's how I got to be a preacher. Not quite as I envisioned it would be.

I never did start that church in Montreal. After a few frustrating months with the Coles, the general headquarters in Canada invited me to begin a mission church in the little community of Woodstock. The denomination had rented an old, run-down church building and parsonage. They had contacted about a dozen interested people in the community. Their plan, however, had been to install a young married couple, thinking this would be necessary for this work. So I married in response to this need, shortening my courtship.

It was real and sacrificial love for my young bride, Dorothy, to plunge into this work with me. We got to Woodstock with no welcome whatsoever. The parsonage was a sprawling house with enough discards in furniture for us to put a single piece in every room. We arrived amid a brutal northern winter with snow drifts almost second-story high. The bitter cold tempted me more than once to use that furniture for firewood.

The abandoned church was actually rather impressive on the outside with its stone front and stained-glass windows. But inside, it was antiquated and totally without heat.

The only possible auditorium was deep in the bowels of the church where the little pot-bellied stove stood. So it was there that I began to apply my Bible school training. It would turn out to be mostly unlearning— discovering how things were, instead of how they were supposed to be.

I expected the people to be enthusiastic and hungry for my "brilliant" exegesis of the Scriptures and new revelations. But what they talked about were Dorothy's good looks, the temperature of the room, Piggy's odor and how hard it was to get to church. Years later, I met one of those first parishioners and with a little chuckle, the gentleman said, "You know, C.M., you couldn't preach in those days. But you cried a lot."

He was right. This morning was no different. I was having to scream just to keep half the congregation from dozing. And I dreaded ending the service. Piggy would be among the first to greet me. Then it would be all over. Somehow, she thought that by clasping my hand, through some kind of osmosis, she could get a spiritual blessing. By the time I could free my hand, it would be filthy and I would be too sick from odor to speak to anyone else.

But this morning, I discovered something eternally valuable. I found that by beating her to the draw, I could wrap my fingers around hers, greet her and yet be free to release her hand at any time and scoot away.

This particular discovery has been a continual blessing to me for the more than fifty years I've spent in the preaching ministry. Preaching and pastoring are people-oriented ministries. To be effective, a pastor must devote himself to his people—not becoming ensnared or enslaved by them, but freely serving them from the heart.

Come to think of it, that *is* perhaps what I learned best in Bible school—something about people.

2

Bible School

The old adage says (and I firmly believe in it and teach it) that a young man goes to Bible school to find a wife. Well, it didn't happen that way for me—not that I didn't try.

I think it was just that the girls saw too much green behind my ears. And there were other stumbling blocks as well.

The first one was my roommate in the dorm. God had to be with me in those Bible school years or I would have killed him for sure.

One of the best ways to gain status and impress the girls (or at least so I thought) was through the dorm room contests. They were intramural competitions for the best-looking rooms. The girls would judge the rooms every Saturday morning and give out prizes. I got some carpeting and pictures and really tried to do it up right.

Well, come Saturday morning, my gallant, young roommate would disappear from the room as though it had the plague. If he didn't need to go to the doctor, he'd have an appointment with the car mechanic or something else. I'd be left to clean the carpet, dust the room and pick up his stuff. If it is possible to have an allergy to physical work, this guy had it.

So he became a very valuable instrument of God's

grace in teaching me patience and tolerance—perhaps more than all the text study I did on those subjects.

There were others in the dorm who played an important role in my education. Dad was definitely a holiness preacher. As pastor of the denomination's headquarters church in Springfield, he implanted more than a healthy respect in me for proper adherence to rules and standards of the church. In short, I was a "goody-goody."

And it was my dorm mates who largely taught me that a "goody-goody" can be "good for nothing," especially when it comes to pastoring God's people. It is the kid who puts the detergent into the school fountain, who once he's guided in the right direction, becomes the guy who will make it on the mission field. The person who is so proper and right that he can't let his humanity show probably won't make it.

The Bible says that salt without savor is good for nothing but to be trampled under foot. Well, fortunately there were plenty of "savory" guys in our dorm, who always had a way of bringing out our humanity whether we liked it or not.

One of the best incidents happened during my first year. A colleague in the dorm rose early one morning and gathered six pairs of shoes which he arranged very neatly behind the doors of all the toilets in the men's lavatory. So with the rising bell, most of us, as usual, broke from our dorms racing to the lavatory.

We were surprised to see every booth filled. Minutes went by and no one left. Nature was pushing us to despair. Finally after about fifteen minutes, one of the guys said, "In the name of the Trinity, if one of you don't come out soon I'm going to force the door open and haul you out."

A few frustrating minutes later, he did just that—and those shoes went a flying!

And we began to discover that God is not a monotone—that those seated on the platform should express some humanity. The stark stereotype of the classic clergyman with his stern look, severe dress and intoning platitudes is a long way from the One who came in the flesh and loved to pick up babies. Those babies weren't always dry and they would often run their sticky fingers through His beard. Jesus was also a popular dinner guest and He was even accused of being a winebibber and a glutton. Our Lord showed us it is a blend of the human and the spiritual that creates great ministry.

It was that same blend that filled the great professors in our Bible school training. The pedagogues who stood before the class and just recited mechanically were quickly forgotten. We could have used the library to get the same information.

True education flows out of association. Someone has coined this truth—education is not taught but caught. Jesus understood this by taking twelve men to be *with* Him. Rough, ignorant and poor-mannered, they learned principally by watching Jesus. Jesus taught primarily by example. He declared, "Because I live, ye shall live also" (John 14:19). Similarly, the teachers who had a life-changing impact on us in Bible school were those who translated something real from the depths of their souls.

George Kerr was such a man. We fondly called him Daddy Kerr, not because he reduced us to children but in a true sense he discipled us to Jesus. There was never a question of how much Jesus meant to him. He treasured every day as an opportunity to help us get to know Jesus better.

Daddy Kerr's zeal for living and learning was contagious. His life radiated the truth that God's richness is an unsearchable mystery—simple enough to be comprehended by a little child and yet so deep and full that it will take us all eternity to fully know our Creator.

Over against the zealous spiritual wisdom of Daddy Kerr was the exactness of Mrs. Frank Boyd. Yes, she taught the mechanics of accurate English, but she taught it directly from her heart. She recognized the power of words "fitly spoken" and demonstrated the majesty of proper English.

Like a musical instrument finely tuned or a tool sharply hewn, exactness in grammar can cause words to cut sharp and deep into the soul to bring about the intended transformation. Much of the fruit of my twenty-five years of radio ministry must be attributed to Mrs. Boyd's diligence.

My earthly parent, elder A.G. Ward, also taught us at Central Bible Institute. He was the master of homiletics and taught us that you must have a game plan for every message you give. Heaven help your audience if you don't know where you're going.

Dad taught us that anything accomplished for the Kingdom of God in this world required human effort as well as divine inspiration and guidance. There is no victory without a battle. He would say, "It takes grit as well as grace to sing praises at midnight. Now 'grit' is not a very pretty word but it denotes an excellent quality. It is that precentage of iron in a man's temperament that gives stablility and permanence to his character—a steel rod in his backbone."

The blend of backgrounds of all our teachers also added to our education at CBI. Dad had been Methodist,

Daddy Kerr was Presbyterian, and Mrs. Boyd was from the Christian and Missionary Alliance. From them, we received a bigger, broader picture of our great God, just as is happening today through the charismatic movement.

And we saw Him in real and genuine servants. For that I am eternally grateful.

3

Dorothy

I did meet Dorothy, my bride of fifty years, during those Bible school years, but not while I was at Springfield.

The summer months after my second year of Bible school I had gone into Kansas to do a little practice preaching. Having the call of God is one thing but learning the art of preaching is another.

Why the Lord picked an opening in Kansas was beyond me. In the whole state there was only one piece of pavement which ran from the University in Lawrence to Kansas City. The rest of the state was just wide open spaces and dust or mud trails, depending on the weather.

My invitation had come from a little backwoods town called Ottawa. When I arrived, I inquired at the general store about the location of the church. The storekeeper replied, "Oh, you mean Holy Joe's root house down by Skunk River."

Perhaps, the difficulty in getting to Ottawa provided fortitude or I would have turned around and left immediately. It turned out that Holy Joe was Mr. Fred Bogler, who later became assistant general superintendent of our denomination. Fred was originally from Australia but had settled in Ottawa in hopes of opening the state of Kansas to the full gospel message.

I made my way to the Boglers to find that the sanctuary was in the little concrete basement he'd built under his house, which lay beside a flood plain called Skunk Run. Fred and his wife warmly welcomed me but had no place for me to stay. There were no cabins or motels in those days, and I could not have afforded one if there were.

Fred told me, "Don't worry, son, we'll find you a 'prophet's chamber' somewhere." And before long, he did. I learned that most people, if they had a spare room, welcomed a preacher, believing that God would bring a blessing to their home through his presence.

So I found an abode with the Hymes family. The Hymes had been brought to Jesus through one of Billy Sunday's sermons that had been printed on the front page of the *Kansas City Star*. Having come to Christ, they looked for a church to attend and found fellowship in the Church of the Nazarene. Unfortunately, the local pastor had taken offense at a very inconsequential thing.

The oldest daughter of the Hymes family had recently graduated from high school and was now attending college in Ottawa, but continued wearing her simple high school class ring. The pastor, speaking from the pulpit, declared this was intolerable—that the wearing of any ornament was contrary to the holiness of the church. Understandably, the family left the church, hurt and shamed.

When I arrived, therefore, the Hymes family was without a church home. At the time they had two unmarried daughters. I first met Dorothy, the younger of the two.

Dorothy was quite a popular young woman in town. She was bright, a fine soloist and musician, and athletically inclined. I was immediately impressed and interested. But I had competition, the strongest coming from a young Baptist minister she was dating at the time.

I was thrilled when Dorothy said she wanted to hear me preach, even if she was going to bring her Baptist friend along. At the time, I only had three sermons—my testimony, one good message and a rather mediocre one. So this night I was going to preach my real good sermon.

Everything went fine. I got into the big moment of the message, which was the confrontation of the Lord with Saul at Damascus. I made it very dramatic, having Saul riding a horse about the size of Marshal Dillon's in "Gunsmoke." In my mind, this burning light shone, the divine voice spoke and Saul fell right out of the saddle. I made it a real Hollywood production with all the theatrics I could muster.

Afterwards, the young Baptist minister came up and said, "That was a remarkable message, Mr. Ward. That bit about the horse especially interests me. I have trained in seminary and I can't seem to remember a horse."

I brashly replied before all, "That's the trouble with you Baptists. You don't go far enough. You need the full gospel to bring you a full revelation of the truth."

"Well," he said, "I'd like to include that part in my preaching. Would you be kind enough to show it to me?"

I opened up the book of Acts and that horse was nowhere to be found. It had been born in my imagination. I was so embarrassed. I wanted to find that skunk hole quick and hide.

But it taught me an important lesson both in preaching and in life. You must guard against the strongholds of your imagination, as Paul says in 2 Corinthians 10. Pride cometh before a fall every time.

There went my good sermon and all I had left was me and mediocrity. I thought I was done for—at least as far as Dorothy was concerned. But Dorothy even then, had the wisdom to see that what makes a real man is not that he doesn't fail, but how he reacts to life when he does.

The advantages I received from living in her home gradually overcame my shortcomings and the competition. A little piece of advice from my mother helped me along. She said, "If you see the girl you want to marry, don't lose any time. But don't tell your father I said so." Dad was so wary of Bible school girls that I think he'd hoped I'd be celibate. The Bible, rather, encourages, "Whoso findeth a wife findeth a good thing" (Prov. 18:22).

Dorothy and I courted for nearly three years. It would have been longer had not my first pastorate called for the service of a married couple. God has a gentle way of prodding when we lack courage and fortitude.

A few imaginations also went out the window with the promises of what kind of home I was going to make for Dorothy. The winter we arrived in Woodstock after our honeymoon was the year of the stock market crash and the Great Depression. The whole economy was in shambles. We had been promised financial help from general headquarters but it never arrived.

Many large questions filled our minds that first winter: Why were we here? Why did we have to start our married life and ministry at this dreadful time? What could we possibly accomplish having so little ourselves? Theological dissertations in answer to these questions were hollow. We needed solid answers and heartfelt assurance. The solution was, of course, in looking up: "I will lift up mine eyes unto the hills, from whence cometh my help. My help cometh from the Lord, which made heaven and earth" (Ps. 121:1, 2).

We found our security was in knowing and doing His

will. That required employing all our resources—spirit, mind, and body. God's Word says to strive to be "not slothful in business; fervent in spirit; serving the Lord" (Rom. 12:11).

Our prayers were not to become more pious or "spiritual" or to be used to more excellently exegete the Scriptures but they were to be almost desperate pleas to bring us into total harmony with His will and plan that we might literally survive. When in those trials God brought His peace and assurance to our hearts, we knew He had heard and would answer.

Our prayers began to take on "feet." And our efforts began to have His guidance and direction. Divine fervency is that prayerful expectancy that God's loving answer is on its way. Just as God provided Elijah with a little woman in the time of famine, He provided Dorothy and me an energetic Canadian hungry for God, one of the few townspeople who had employment.

I was able to lead this young man to Christ and see him filled with the Spirit. He became our star boarder for five dollars a week. This is what we lived on the first year of our married life and ministry.

After that, I wrote a short note to general headquarters: "If and when you are able to send us any support, please don't. I might as well discover right now whether there is a real God or not. If God has indeed called me and He is my heavenly Father, He knows what I have need of and I must learn the lessons of trusting Him."

That step of faith, though brash, was perhaps the best one I would make in my young ministry. Learning God's provision was an education in itself. And God never failed to provide. The experience built resoluteness of heart and mind to know that where God guides He can also provide.

And Dorothy and I sure needed His guidance those first few years of adjustment in the ministry.

4

Culture Shock

I've heard it said that the first years of a young preacher's ministry are harder on the congregation than the pastor. If that were true in my case, some wouldn't have survived, because there were times that Dorothy and I didn't think we would.

For one thing, Dorothy's parents were business people, so she was unfamiliar with ministry life, and Canada itself was an adjustment. Dorothy had never been to Canada and soon learned that although Canadians speak English, it's not always the same language.

On her first visit to the general store with her meager shopping list, she asked for crackers. The storekeeper replied, "You want what?"

Dorothy repeated her request, "Crackers, please."

The proprietor looked indignant and said, "Madam, we don't carry crackers in the middle of January." (He supposed she was speaking of firecrackers and poor Dorothy had no idea she should be asking for soda biscuits.)

Being born and raised in Canada, the culture was less of a shock for me than learning to deal with parishioners as human beings. With anguish, I learned that outside of the Bible, nothing is sacred. It is all up for review.

That first year, through sheer determination, I had

built a small congregation. Scraping together the support of our little band, we were able to leave that musty basement and move into a downtown store building which was more attractive and could seat a couple of hundred people. Amidst the depression around us, we were able to grow to where at least we were paying the rent, fuel, utilities and giving some out to the poor and needy among us.

After working like that and preaching my heart out, one Sunday a parishioner rose and verbally blasted me. He said, "That was so bad! If you were not a preacher, I'd slug you and shut you up."

In that moment, everything within me wanted just to pack it in and walk out the back door. The whole situation seemed hopeless. But faith knows only one direction—*forward*. It is said of Israel, "They journeyed from . . . the wilderness . . . toward the sunrising" (Num. 21:11).

A preacher is no less susceptible to the ups and downs of life than anyone else. He is never more popular than the last good sermon he preaches. Let God bless you and you can hardly leave the building. The people want Bibles and autographs. They want your counsel to their sons and daughters. They invite you home for dinner. But if you have a rough time behind the pulpit, you could drive a jeep down that same aisle.

It's like baseball. You are either a hero or a heel. If you slug a home run, the crowd is on its feet; if you strike out with the bases full, nobody knows you.

It is precisely this challenge of adversity that God is pleased to use to build great men. Joseph is a classic example from the Scriptures of how God allows adversity, injustice and suffering to build the characters of His servants and leaders.

That building of character takes time and most congregations sense that, even if they don't understand it. Just like a pregnancy, there is a time factor that cannot be forced. One must live with it and *wait*.

Surely, one of the hardest things to learn in life is patience, to not dig up those "seedling potatoes" we plant in life, but to watch carefully and wait until the fruit is fully ripe. I believe that, at approximately forty years of age, a person is ready to fulfill the job for which he or she has been sent into the world. Before forty, the time is an investment in preparation. Our later years are coupon-clipping years—the payoff, the reward.

Just so, a pastor must be prepared to make an investment in his congregation—three years at least. I found out from my congregation there in Woodstock that they were not going all out for any young preacher until they knew for sure he intended to stay. Their rationale went something like this:

> First year—pretty kitty
> Second year—poor kitty
> Third year—scat

Nevertheless, I stayed. And in doing so, I learned to obey Paul's injunction, "Having done all, to stand" (Eph. 6:13). And God honored it and brought great peace and blessing to the church.

Really, I should have said, "We stood." Because Dorothy was my greatest encouragement, fan and supporter during those trying times. I came to appreciate the wisdom of general headquarters in asking for a couple, rather than an individual, to take the church.

The great Bill Klem, traditionally the monarch of

major league umpires, gave similar advice to an aspiring umpire after asking, "Are you married?"

"No, I am not, Mr. Klem," the young fellow replied.

Klem responded, "Then get married! You will need someone to love you and have faith in you when you come back from the ballpark where everyone has been against you."

If a pastor (even more than an umpire) wasn't required to withstand heat and hassles from his people, Jesus wouldn't have described the mark of a good shepherd or pastor as one who "giveth his life for the sheep." On the other hand, the hireling "leaveth the sheep and fleeth."

The one *leads* and *protects*; the other *pushes* and *deserts*. The one faces trouble; the other runs from trouble. The one carries a burden; the other hasn't any.

Those first years taught me how to pastor and how to have a burden. I learned that it was the "burdens" that produced my sermons—so I was no longer left with mediocrity.

5

Fisherman or Bounty Hunter?

When I say that in my first years of ministry I was the
worst bushwhacker who ever embarrassed God, you
have to understand a little of my strict holiness upbringing. We walked in such dread of God's wrath, that we
could hardly breathe for fear of taking in sin stains.

When I first parted my hair at the age of fifteen,
Mother was sure that worldliness had grasped hold of
my life. On Sundays we wouldn't eat warm meals
because cooking on the Sabbath was considered to be a
sin. Dad shaved just before midnight Saturday so he
wouldn't have to on the Lord's Day.

However righteous and well-intended were my parents'
beliefs about the Sabbath, I have come to believe they
missed God's best intention for the Lord's Day. Their
whole focus on Sundays was self-denial; I believe God's
focus for it is evangelism.

Before Christ went to Calvary's cross, Israel was
fenced all about by strict laws and rituals. To fail or miss
the mark of any law was to bring on fear, condemnation
and degradation. But the victory that Christ won for us
there is total freedom. We can stumble and even fail,
knowing that Jesus died for sinners and failures. He will
pick us up again and lead us on. To deny the victory of
Calvary is to return to the Dark Ages of legalism.

The great apostle Paul fought as hard against legalism as he did against loose morals or any other sin. In fact, some of his severest words were to the "foolish Galatians," (Gal. 3:1) who had slipped back into legalism. He reminds them that if right standing with God could possibly come by obedience to laws, then Christ's death was totally in vain.

So Sunday, the day of resurrection must be celebrated by freedom—freedom to serve as Christ served—service not for pay, but given freely out of a joyful, grateful heart.

Paul told Timothy that the law remains for the unrighteous, to prevent excess and license. But for the committed believer, life celebrated to its fullest on the Lord's Day is to be lived and shared with much activity and service to both God and our fellowman. The freedom that Christ won for us at Calvary must be proclaimed.

This was, however, not my understanding of God as a teen-ager. I viewed Him as the great Supreme Court Justice who causes us to walk a dangling tightrope over the precipice of hell. This gave me little "room" to help others in the way. Instead, if anybody looked like he could possibly cause me to stumble, I shot him down quickly.

I actually looked for people to send to hell. If a woman had one wave in her hair, she promptly went there because you could not serve Jesus without having your hair straight back in a pilgrim's knot. When I discovered a boy playing marbles, I said immediately, "Oh, a potential gambler. This juvenile is heading straight to hell."

But somewhere along the way during our time in Woodstock, I bumped into John 3:17 which read:

> For God sent not his Son into the world to condemn the world; but that the world through him might be saved.

I discovered that in Christ my feet were not on a tightrope, but on the solid rock, so I could help hurting, sinful people without fear of falling down myself. I got into the salvation business instead of the damnation business. And I haven't sent anyone to hell in forty-eight years.

It is significant that Jesus called us to be fishers of men, not hunters. Hunting implies bullets; fishing implies bait.

In my teens, I looked at myself more as the fish than the fisherman—always afraid to look at or enjoy anything nice or attractive for fear it would be Satan's bait.

As a preacher, a fisherman for Christ, I began to learn it is important to bait the hook of the gospel. It can and must be made attractive—in contrast, I must say, to most of the sermons we heard in Bible school. Perhaps one of the best (and most hated) rules in Bible school was mandatory attendance at chapel. Having to sit and listen to all those "sermons" gave us some comprehension of what a congregation experiences. I decided there had to be a better way to reach people besides just screaming. And one summer, with a little help from Dorothy, I got a clue.

We attended a state fair and I was amazed at the way Dorothy fell under the spell of the pitchmen there. They could be selling anything from a kitchen knife to a clip-on tie. It wasn't the product, it was the appeal. Once they identified themselves with the audience's experience (whether it be chopping onions or trying to tie a tie) the audience was hooked. They had captured the market—all that was left was to reel it in.

That understanding sent me out into the streets to find a market for the gospel. I began to understand more clearly why Jesus spent time in the marketplace and associated with sinners. He went to where the market was and so He sends us.

General Ralph E. Haines, Jr. understood this when he would leave word for the chaplains under his command to leave their office doors open—not so much for others to find them as for them to go out and find others.

Jesus' testimony is our example: "For the Son of man is come to seek and to save that which was lost" (Luke 19:10). Jesus didn't live out His ministry behind some sacred ivory tower but among the common people, circulating throughout the mainstream of human struggles, suffering, and joy. "Jesus went about all the cities and villages, teaching. . . and preaching. . . and healing" (Matt. 9:35).

Jesus' challenge to His disciples is an indictment to many today: "Then shall they also answer him, saying, Lord, when saw we thee an hungred, or athirst, or a stranger, or naked, or sick, or in prison, and did not minister unto thee? Then shall he answer them, saying, Verily I say unto you, Inasmuch as ye did it not to one of the least of these, ye did it not to me" (Matt. 25:44, 45).

Before long, we found ourselves among the hungry, thirsty, sick and imprisoned.

6

A Little Madness Goes a Long Way

Before I completed Bible school, my father gave me some advice about recognizing a good preacher. He said, "You can spot him when you see: 1) color coming to his cheeks, 2) fire coming to his eyes, and 3) a ring coming to his voice."

Hard as I tried, this was not the kind of preaching I could conjure up just by thinking and Bible study. It had to be a message given out of a God-inspired burden. Early in my ministry, I began to ask God to give me that kind of a burden. About that time the Lord moved Dorothy and me to a church in Victoria, British Columbia on the Pacific Coast.

This was when we were still in the midst of the Great Depression. The church facility was the upstairs of a fish-and-chips shop down by the wharf, amidst the rowdy throng of sailors and longshoremen. We had to fight the environment just to survive. Stepping over the drunks to get into church gave us a genuine burden to reach this lost sea of humanity.

Only the love of Jesus could give us eyes to see the potential value in reaching these unchurched and rejected members of society. It is said of Michelangelo that he saw the finished statuary in every rough block of marble he selected. We were reminded that with every kindness

25

to each roughneck and drunk, we were doing it "unto Him."

So we took what bait we had available and went a-fishing in the streets. We combined the bright, upbeat religious music of the day and sparkling testimonies. Frequently, this meant challenging Satan's best—the bars, strip shows and night spots of the town. But God helped us to see that our battle was with Satan and not with the sinners who frequented or even operated these sinful establishments.

It was in those sin-filled streets of Victoria that God taught me a quality of the Spirit that can keep you going when plans, organization, faith and all else fails. It is called *madness.*

You don't believe me? Listen to God's Word:

> The prophet is a fool, the spiritual man is mad.
> (Hos. 9:7)

"Madmen" are those who have changed the world.

It was madness to remove propellers from airplanes. But a jet is better. It was madness to look for penicillin in mold. But it has saved millions of lives.

It was madness in General McAuliffe that saved Eisenhower's armies at the Bulge, when General Rundstedt and the Nazis were breaking through the Ardennes. Completely surrounded at Bastogne and without supplies or air cover, the general replied, "Nuts!" to the German ultimatum to surrender.

Paul was accused of madness. "Paul, thou art beside thyself; much learning doth make thee mad" (Acts 26:24).

They said Jesus was mad. The religious leaders said,

"He hath a devil, and he is mad; why hear ye him?" (John 10:20). Only "insanity" would walk on water. Only madness would touch lepers.

And there were many of my ecclesiastical "friends" who called us crazy to go out and mingle with the drunks and navy "bums" on the streets of Victoria. And except for the power of God's Spirit, we were indeed crazy.

One particular Saturday night when I couldn't find any musical help to come along, I went out into the streets, looking for some way to attract a crowd to whom I could present the claims of Christ.

God used one of the "other side" for my bait. While I was trying without success to stir up a crowd, an alcoholic wandered up to me with his umbrella opened above him on this warm, clear and cloudless night.

This fellow was pleasantly inebriated but not violent. I let him take my arm as he bellowed out—off-key—an old-fashioned hymn. Instead of resisting him, I took advantage of the attention and joined him in a duet. Our unique, comical combination brought a crowd like wildfire. Conveniently, he soon untangled himself and left, allowing me opportunity to begin a message of salvation to all who had gathered.

Another evening we decided to serenade all of the saloons in the city. I rented a large flatbed trailer, put a very noisy—if not smooth—orchestra on the truck and headed down the city streets into the night life.

When we arrived in front of the first saloon, there were sailors and B-girls and all kinds of riffraff in front. I had never been in one of those nightclubs before so I entered cautiously.

When I finally located the manager, I blurted out, "Sir, we have a Christian group of singers and orchestra on a flatbed outside. I'd like your permission for us to strike up the music and play outside your club."

I'll never forget his reaction.

He set his jaw and said to me, "Reverend, if the law permits, it's fine with me. You know, preacher, I really respect you. You are the first person in your world, the church, to come where we are and challenge what we are doing."

I asked further, "Would you have any objection if we were to play as close to the front door as possible?"

He replied, "No, I have no objection. I always wanted to see what would happen to men and women of the cocktail crowd—the dancing crowd—in the midst of the gospel."

When we began to play and sing the gospel, it was like magic. The drinking stopped; the dancing stopped; and the bar emptied. Many people left the nightclub first to see what was happening. Others departed to find another bar where this challenge wasn't present, because darkness can hardly exist where there is light. But others were hooked and saved that night.

The local newspaper had fun with it but gave us free publicity, featuring a full picture of myself and the musicians with a headline that read, "Pentecostal Pastor Serenades Nightclubs." For that, I was called on the religious carpet. But following the advice of a close friend who said, "Don't apologize—your enemies won't believe you and your friends don't need it," I stood my ground and went on.

And this is what I discovered as I pastored those wonderful, hurting people of Victoria: If God has made you the leader, He will give you the strength and courage to stand. You don't quit and give up. "And having done all, to stand" (Eph. 6:13).

And how these people needed someone to stand up for them to let them know that their lives, their eternal souls, were worth fighting for and struggling over after so many others had put them down and rejected them. How I love a line from the book of Hebrews, "He ever liveth to make intercession for them" (Heb. 7:25). Jesus not only gave His life for our sins but He is still battling, interceding to help us conquer sin.

There were times in the church of Victoria that I preached when I was so sick and in so much pain, I couldn't see the people in the front rows. My fleshly nature would cry out to give it up and argue that it wasn't worth all the struggle. But then a face would shine through the blur and its eyes would say, "Pastor, you do care that I make it. You're in there helping me battle sin and Satan, so I am going to try and fight." And suddenly, a new surge of strength would lift me onward.

The fire and the color came as we battled for eternal souls—they had been rejected by many, yes, but they were still ones for whom Christ suffered and died. Should we do less?

7

Resilience

The previous chapter on madness is true but it must be tempered and balanced or we'll all wind up killing ourselves, or one another. There is a world of difference between trying to work a miracle for God and allowing God to work a miracle through you.

In my study, I keep before me a prominent figurine of Don Quixote to remind myself not to charge at windmills. History is already strewn with broken lances.

Yes, you may be called to add your name to *Foxe's Book of Martyrs*. But don't look forward to it unless heaven destines it to be so.

There is a marked difference between a God-given objective and presumption. Most often, experience is the only reliable teacher.

Early in my ministry, soon after I had taken a job as the editor of the denomination's magazine in Canada, I was fired—for attending a professional hockey game. Before God called me to preach, I'd always wanted to be a hockey player.

The general council, declaring that such attendance was worldly and improper, brought me before a full ecclesiastical court. Before they reached their decision, I stood up and declared, "Gentlemen, my conscience will not allow me to admit I'm wrong. If such actions were prohibited in my contract and I agreed to it, fine. But to impose conscience upon me without setting forth your convention and rules, I think is very unfair." I was right—dead right—and thereby got my walking papers. For the Christian, the end never justifies the means. The means is how we get to eternal life. One of the trials of our faith is learning to choose the thing of eternal value over the immediate gain.

After that, I began to learn that being right doesn't mean you always win. To win without God is to lose. So soon after my hockey experience, God gave me another chance to learn about resilience and moderation.

I had been asked to pastor a large church and God was richly blessing our efforts. We were growing, but the church building was large and had plenty of space. So it seemed the perfect solution when a nearby church with similar doctrine wanted to close its doors and join our fellowship.

They had thousands of dollars worth of assets and great talent and enthusiasm in their body of believers. However, the two churches were so close together that both could not prosper, so they wanted to liquidate. I believed strongly this was God's will and moved to set up all the arrangements. But when it came to a vote, my board decided it would not be in the church's best interest.

I was furious and embarrassed. The other church was embarrassed. My self-nature wanted to charge San Juan Hill and fight. But this time, I checked my spirit and there was no release.

Sunday morning I stepped to the platform and declared, "I submit to both the intelligence and the number of fine men with whom I serve. I appreciate their viewpoint even though mine is different. Because of their unanimity and dedication to the same God I serve, they must be correct and I accept their decision."

It built that entire congregation's respect for me so much that, in reality, I gained far more than I lost.

Receiving that mandate of spiritual authority and establishing oneself in that place does not mean that a pastor will or even should win all the "battles" in the church. You can be defeated occasionally and still not lose. A pastor's success here will often depend on his resilience.

The Japanese, with their admirable genius and culture, give us a picture of resilience. The symbol that describes them best is *bamboo,* not *steel.* Steel has a point of stress. It can collapse. Bamboo bends. It will lay over before hurricane strength. When the storm abates, bamboo rights itself.

There is a great lesson in this: *Flexibility is a strength, not a weakness.*

The Japanese bow tells us more. The Japanese people never bow too high to be insolent and never too low to be subservient.

Corporate strength, whether it be found in business or in the church, is massive. To take it on single-handedly is usually a sign of paranoia. *Bow politely before the storm!* Like our Japanese friends, as you bend at just the right angle, say "I am so sorry." Then revive and continue.

Otherwise, you'll be broken.

In fact, in the Bible school classes I've taught recently, I tell all the aspiring pastors, "If you want to survive long in any one church, then twice a year from the pulpit, admit you are wrong. The congregation will love you for it and will welcome you back to the human race."

Dr. Norman Vincent Peale does this brilliantly by sharing a little humor about himself. He will begin his message to the congregation by saying, "Can you hear me comfortably? I am sorry Mrs. Peale is not here. She usually monitors the sound level for me from where she sits in the audience. If I am too loud, she will go like this (and he plugs his ears with his fingers to show her reaction). If I am not speaking loudly enough, she will do this (and he cups his ears, showing how she indicates strain in hearing). But recently she has been going like this (and he pinches his nose)."

It's uncomfortable for people to live with perfection. Perfect people tend to disappear. "And Enoch . . . was not; for God took him" (Gen. 5:24). I've checked the records and, at least in our denomination, we haven't lost anyone like that—clergy or laity—since incorporation.

It's also uncomfortable to *pose,* to project an image that you are better than you really are. Don't play God!

Listen to Jesus' words: "Learn of me; for I am meek and lowly in heart: and ye shall find rest" (Matt. 11:29). "Condescend to men of low estate. Be not wise in your own conceits" (Rom. 12:16). *Be approachable!*

If one recent American president had practiced an attitude of fallibility and humanness, he would have likely escaped ignominy.

Getting back to the outgrowth of being fired from my job at Canadian general headquarters, it turned out to be a great blessing. So much so that, though I don't make it a general rule, I do advocate that everyone get fired at least once in a lifetime. And not because as the saying goes, "It helps you make up your mind."

I believe being fired or experiencing some form of

failure can cause a person, as it did for me, to entrust one's whole life afresh to God and to find a new dimension of His grace—to face the worst and walk right through it in Christ to victory. To learn that the heavens won't fall and the earth doesn't open up to swallow you just because you've been fired is an important lesson. I think the best line I heard on this was by the great Yale football coach Herman Hickman, who said, "When you're being fired or thrown out, get to the head of the line and look like you're leading the parade."

I have been fired from positions three times in my life. Each time there were some hurts for Dorothy and myself, but never for long. In fact, my relations with those who fired me in every case have since greatly strengthened and deepened in love.

For example, just recently I joined "PTL Club" President Jim Bakker on the campus of North Central Bible College in Minneapolis to open the new chapel (for which I had raised funds). "PTL Club" was televising the event and Jim asked me to preach the service. In introducing me, he said, "C.M., am I correct in saying you were fired from this campus?"

It hit my funny bone and I laughed, "Yes, yes, Jim, I was, and the man who fired me is right down here. I've just been sitting with him." This was my wonderful friend, Frank Lindquist, who had been college president and district superintendent when my services at that campus had been terminated.

The bottom line is this: you can get knocked around and beaten down, but if Jesus is in your ship, no matter how bad the storm, it's not going to sink. And Jesus in you is not going to stop loving people. God is crazy about people.

8

Learning What's Important

My experience in Victoria gave me a burden for souls but I had to learn that it isn't the numbers won that is important, it is the eternal value of each human soul for whom Christ died.

I became acutely aware of this truth in an unforgettable experience in 1944, right in the midst of the World War II drama. An evangelistic endeavor in the city of Battle Creek, Michigan, had invited me to come for a soul-winning crusade. The rallies were very effective and I enjoyed considerable success as an evangelist.

A dear friend at that time was a highly placed executive with the Kellogg Company. He approached me about joining some company executives who were invited to be guests at a certain learning exercise at nearby Camp Custer.

The military were busy training military police for mop-up operations in Sicily and Italy. The need for special training was apparent. Snipers, enemy partisan troops and guerrilla action would infest the cities as the Germans and Italians retreated and Americans and Allies advanced. These pockets of resistance had to be cleaned out by specially trained military police.

The training exercises were conducted by battle-hardened drill instructors. Mock streets had been built and recruits were learning to take cover under live ammunition. The scenes were realistic.

Suddenly, a hand was laid on my shoulder. A lieutenant asked me to follow him. I thought at first I might be asked to leave because of my status. However, this was not the intent of the interruption.

The lieutenant led me across the parade ground toward a permanent building. Soon I understood his mission. I could hear the fearful sounds from behind barred windows. Scores of wrecked minds had been brought from the first terrible hand-to-hand fighting in Guadalcanal. These were the living dead. They were screaming and, hour after hour, reliving the terrors of a newer kind of warfare that the Japanese had introduced into the jungles of Asia and the Pacific. I braced myself for this experience.

The lieutenant led me into the foyer of the administration building. Suddenly I was face to face with a full colonel. He was a West Point graduate and regular army. He was also a qualified medical doctor. Here I was to learn the most important lesson of my ministry, taught by a strange instructor, but handpicked by providence.

At the time I was very professional, and tragically ambitious. I was concerned about my advancement, name, pulpit, level and popularity. These, however, were to be crucified within ten minutes.

I made the tactical mistake of implying to the colonel that unfortunately his assignment would not create any headlines for him. I wanted to sympathize with him. He was administering a building filled with human wreckage. It seemed to me to be so obscure, hopeless, and an assignment in which a man must be forgotten.

"Hey," the colonel said, "You may or may not think I

am religious. It really doesn't matter a great deal. I believe that in the book called the Bible there is a word, 'lost.' These lads, hundreds of them under my command, are lost. They have as much right to live as you have, sir. I want them to live. That is my goal.

"The day may arrive, God grant it be continued, that a mother may stand where you are standing, and one of these crazed lads be led into her presence and suddenly a miracle take place. It will be a miracle in which the lad suddenly returns from a dark and evil world that imprisons him, to a world of recognition and I can hear the boy say, 'Mother' and hear the mother say, 'Son,' and I will have been rewarded far more than if I were to win medals and ribbons."

I stood speechless in front of the colonel. In that one moment, this military man had brought me all the way back to point zero. I had not realized until then how far I had drifted from my own calling and commitment. Like King David in his tragic census of Israel, I had begun to count pews, parking lots, buildings, newspaper publicity, auditoriums and what I thought was success.

David, God's special friend, got into more trouble when he became involved in numbers' games than for any other transgression. One passage says, "And David said unto God, I have sinned greatly, because I have done this thing" (1 Chron. 21:8).

God had given Israel a pattern for taking a census. "When thou takest the sum of the children of Israel after their number, then shall they give every man a ransom of his soul unto the Lord, when thou numberest them; that there be no plague among them, when thou numberest them" (Exod. 30:12).

God never looks upon mankind as digits, ZIP codes or

merchandise. They are always living souls. David ignored this and brought calamity upon Israel. Now God was trying to spare me this same calamity.

Quickly, I searched for a private place to repent, cry and pray, thanking God for His abundant mercy. Since then I have never forgotten that each and every human being is an eternal soul, worth my greatest trust and efforts on an individual basis.

Numbers are inconsequential. They are a bonus given and never a goal sought. Whether in the census for Israel (where every man counted had to have a ransom for his soul) or in the ghettos of New York, God never looks upon mankind as digits, ZIP codes or merchandise.

They are always individual, living souls. And His Spirit goes to and fro seeking to find one He may win and deliver.

Experiencing this truth in the depths of my soul had a life-changing effect on my ministry.

9

God's Many-Splendored Salvation

The Apostle Paul described the gospel as a "mystery" and the "unsearchable riches of Christ." Sharing a task so wonderful and so vast, makes a pastor's job exciting, challenging and, yes, sometimes trying.

There are an infinite number of ways to share the simple message of God's salvation; there are an infinite number of things in which we can see God's power and His goodness; and there are an infinite variety of people and instruments through which He has chosen to express himself.

How anyone could be alive and say God is dead is beyond me.

Jesus had a marvelous ability to see God in everything. He understood the fullness of God, the Creator. He saw God's footstep and plan in everything from the lilies to the lepers.

As God led Dorothy and me in pastorates from one part of Canada to another and then from the Midwest to Bakersfield, California, we basked in the beautiful variety of both God's creation and His people.

My sermons began to change. Bible school theories and theology gave way to God's nursery school discoveries: to see in nature, the mirror of God; to study the hummingbird, deemed impossible to fly by all laws of flying, yet among the most graceful of birds. How amazing and delightful the Great Designer is!

This little illustration brought many to acknowledge the reality of God. For if there is design in nature, there must be a designer. If there is a designer, there must be intellect. If there is intellect, there must be a person, a Creator.

I also began to see that words could smile and bring life instead of binding and condemning: "The letter killeth, but the spirit giveth life" (2 Cor. 3:6). Instead of entitling my sermon, "The Doctrine of Eschatology," it became, "Gonna Take a Sentimental Journey." Heaven became not a hazy doctrine for much argumentative discussion. Rather it was the abode of the fullness of God's loving nature—our eternal hope and completion—a moving on from this temporary dwelling place (2 Pet. 1:13) back home to the Creator—a rest, release and reward.

Another time God laid a message of healing on my heart. I called it, "Me and My Shadow" and I drew upon the biblical text where, as Peter walked down the street, his shadow fell on people and they were healed. How well this describes the loving nature of God toward us: "He has showered down upon us the richness of his grace—for how well he understands us and knows what is best for us at all times" (Eph. 1:8, TLB). Healing is perhaps the easiest of all languages to help us understand the love of God. In His divine touch we find the message, *"I love and want your wholeness. I am ready and able to do the same to your soul and spirit if you will but believe."* This is God's grand purpose in divine healing.

When I spoke on God's grace, I entitled the sermon, "The Best Things in Life Are Free." And when I spoke to young people, I would draw on the popular movies and song titles of the day, such as "Love Letters in the Sand," and "Lost Weekend."

Frequently, I found success in drawing on people's God-given curiosity with titles like, "Will You Meet Pontius Pilate in Heaven?"; "A Cure for Heart Trouble"; "Can I Get to Heaven on a Pass?"; and "The Great Tranquilizer."

The *Los Angeles Times* once published a front-page feature and picture of a brutal murder that showed a striking brunette whom they dubbed, "The Black Dahlia." I got a copy of the photo of the girl and ran it in an ad entitled, "The Black Dahlia, or Lily of the Valley?" When I got to church, people were lined up back to the street, waiting to get in.

It became a popular pastime on Saturdays in Bakersfield to get the paper and check the church page to see the latest topic Doctor Ward had come up with.

This kind of advertising backfired on occasions, too. One weekend I was called away on a speaking engagement and the man who normally did the advertising in my absence was away, also. This combination gave ample opportunity to some young pranksters in the church to do us in—but good.

Among the elders in the church at the time was a Mr. Clemo. He was an ardent Christian, but young in the faith and not well-educated or cultured. In his zeal, he would buttonhole and practically force young people to go to the altar after my sermons. He did so with the best of intentions, but it antagonized some of the youth.

So they concocted an ad which read, "Dr. Jake Clemo, Dean of the Chicago Uplifters Society, will begin a new crusade at the Pentecostal Assembly, Sunday night. He will be assisted by the Juvenile Chirpers." Apparently, the editors, so used to my shocking ads, thought it not unusual and, therefore, they published it—much to my chagrin.

But then, humor is also a great part of God's many-splendored salvation. To build a great church, to be a great pulpiteer, one must glean and learn to draw on the widest possible spectrum of God's unsearchable riches.

For instance, some love to preach the gospel of holiness. Others love the gospel of power, miracles, etc. Still others feed constantly on prophecy. However, if they limit their message only to their area of particular interest, they will find their appeal limited to a small audience.

Paul said God's workman is "thoroughly furnished." He is able to learn to proclaim both holiness and mercy, power and prophecy. And if he is not yet thoroughly equipped, he will, at least, be open to surrounding himself with those who are knowledgeable in those areas. In this vein, I so appreciate the testimony of Jim Bakker who says, "PTL was not built on my speaking ability or television expertise: God surrounded me with the best, talented Christians in the field."

Sharing one's pulpit and ministry with others is no easy thing for a pastor. And not without good reason. The platform is fertile ground for crackpots. Nearly every experienced pastor has been burned a time or two.

Our own natural bias is to invite people into our home and pulpit whom we agree with and enjoy. But sometimes God sends us an instrument that is more annoying than anything. And the successful pastor will be open to this kind of godly intrusion.

On a particular occasion in Bakersfield, I was treated to this blessing, and not by my choice. An evangelist was highly recommended to me (by a pastor who, I think, had a problem with him and wanted to unload him at my door). It was during the time when the healing ministry began to be emphasized, and I was told this man had a remarkable healing ministry.

So I invited him and he accepted. Twice within ten days, he was picked up by the State Highway Patrol. Not that he hurt anybody, he was just getting to town, too quickly.

Every night during the song service, he would walk toward a large briefcase, cough and empty its contents. Cradling the stack of papers in his arm before the congregation, he would ramble through it until something attracted him. He would pull out that paper and it would become the sermon for the night.

The first Sunday after he came, he brought a sheet over to me and asked, "I haven't preached this yet, have I?"

"Not to my recollection," I replied.

"You wouldn't double-cross me now, would you?" he bantered.

Then practically every evening sometime during his message, he'd get tired and stop and say, "I just can't preach any more. C.M., you preach." About the time I'd get warmed up to the task, he'd touch me on the shoulder and say, "I feel better now. You can sit down and I'll finish."

The only redeeming talent it seemed he had, was a very good solo voice. But after the first night, he said, "I'm not going to sing. I'm going to play my records." And he'd play this little wind-up phonograph that screeched. Then for the next fifteen minutes he'd pitch his record and say, "Now, God knows when you will get this record. I don't know when it will be mailed to you, but I'd like to have the cash now."

It took every ounce of my restraint to keep from throwing the bum out on his ear. Here I was trying to build a respectable church and I was stuck for two weeks with a fruitcake.

What was it Paul said about the "foolish things of this world"?

The first week this evangelist was with us, three of the leading car dealers of the city were saved. One of them, a sharp man who was an alcoholic, was saved the first thirty seconds of the invitation. He stood and met me at the altar and said, "C.M., I reckon you're going to be my pastor. I've already decided three things. First: I'm never again going to sell a piece of equipment on the Lord's day. Second: I'm going to pay my tithes like I pay my taxes. And third: I don't know what you're driving, but drive it into my place in the morning; I'll have a new piece of equipment waiting for you."

As long as I was his pastor, he provided me with a new car every six months.

The blessings of opening our eyes and broadening our perspectives to God's "unsearchable riches" in His people are limitless.

10

What Price Salvation?

The old adage says, "You get what you pay for." My whole life I have been hoping against hope to prove that wrong.

I still look to try to get a good steak for $4.95. I'm still trying to get a suit that looks like something that a Kennedy would wear for $39.95. But all that I've ever found is that a cheap offer brings cheap results. When tempted to bargain and try to shortcut, my worst cost is the cheap one and my best cost is my first one.

As funny as this is in food and clothes, it is tragically worse in the offering of salvation through Jesus Christ.

Today we see scores of evangelistic merchants in all areas of media offering nothing down and eternity to pay. It may bring good numbers and statistics, but it won't bring a changed life for God's glory.

God has called us to be "workmen that needeth not to be ashamed." If we offer a cheap, empty salvation somewhere down the road (even if it's in eternity), we will meet those people whose lives have been wrecked and hollowed by that misconception. Personally, I don't want to look at a wrecked life and say I was party to that; Jesus calls the end of this—a hell seven times worse than before.

True salvation starts and ends with faith (Rom. 1:17).

God is not opposed to knowledge and intelligence but you cannot start there. It must start with those two most powerful words, "I believe." The fiery, unlearned Apostle Peter put it in its proper perspective. He said, "Add to your faith virtue; and to virtue knowledge" (2 Pet. 1:5).

The vital question in offering salvation is not, "Do you know?", but "Will you believe?" For without faith, it is *impossible* to please God.

This "open-minded hogwash" has even pervaded many of our Christian colleges—putting the emphasis on knowledge, no matter where it leads. The Garden of Eden experience shouts out to us about what a mistake that is. Satan can distort and twist knowledge, but not faith.

Again, God is not opposed to knowledge. Faith grows and is strengthened by uncontestable facts. True investigation and analysis of God's creation explodes and illuminates the truth and glory of God's nature. In biology, in thermodynamics, chemistry, language, sociology—everything—we see design. And if there is design, there must be a designer and therefore a Creator. Spirit-filled teaching will only add to and strengthen faith.

Yet, all the facts and knowledge in the world, without a spirit of faith, will only produce an argument. Jesus said of these, "even though one would raise from the dead, they won't believe. . . ." No, we must start with, "I believe, because it happened to me and therefore it can happen to you, too!"

What is the price of "I know"?

There must be a separation. One cannot be double-willed and double-minded and expect to know. Salvation is not some magical game. It is a new life that is lived on God's terms—and His alone.

It is a contractual relationship, illustrated perhaps best by the one a woman makes to a man in marriage. Here is the sweet, young child all in frills and flowers, friends and froth, heart tumbled out, mouthing "I do" but knowing so little of what it means.

The moment of truth doesn't come until three days later when she discovers he can be a jerk. She cries out, "You monster, who are you to tell me what to do?" And he says, "You swore in God's name to honor and obey—and that includes the laundry and housekeeping."

Jesus is not only our Savior, but He is our Lord and Master. Without taking the whole package, salvation will never work. There are many names used to describe His Lordship—like dedication and sanctification—but whatever you call it, you won't be happy in Jesus until you learn to trust and obey.

There are maybe some "swingers" (idiots) today who will settle for a part-time lover, but not me. I want all of my wife. If I am going to pay the bills, I want full-time service. That is what God wants. He is not going to settle for Sunday mornings and Wednesday evenings. Jesus must be our everything or He is nothing. To put it straight: He is bigger than General Motors; you just don't bargain with Him. You cannot get New Testament benefits without going the New Testament way.

The blessing of this is that when we go God's way, we don't have to wrangle with cigarettes, alcohol and all the other stumbling stones. That's because when He comes in, the other things must go. Salvation is living under new management.

Now Jesus doesn't much care about the condition of the establishment when we turn over the keys. Jesus waded into a thousand devils so He isn't afraid to tackle the mess of our lives when we truly give Him our whole life: "If any man hear . . . and open the door, I will come in" (Rev. 3:20). When we turn over the keys and say, "Yes, Lord," the miracle starts.

There are plenty of merchants who will offer a "better" deal—just make this confession, just follow these rules, just let us dunk you—but the results will show what is really the better offer. Like paying a good price for a suit, when you get true salvation, you look good in it.

In Psalm 4:3 David points out two benefits of true salvation: "But know that the Lord hath set apart him that is godly for himself: the Lord will hear when I call unto him."

The first benefit then is a beautiful sense of reality. Somewhere between the cradle and the grave, we have the privilege of knowing for certain whether there is "anybody up there" or not.

As Paul declares, if we are just serving the figment of someone's imagination, "we are of all men most miserable." If there is just a vacuum out there like the Communists say, we ought to know that. But if there really is a living, all-powerful God, it is the greatest discovery we can ever make.

How do we know that we know? David says, "the Lord will hear me when I call."

Leonard Crimp, a good Canadian friend of mine, gave most of his life to the Heinz Foods Company, working his way up to general sales manager of all Canada. Leonard was also a man of strong and forceful faith, an international leader among the Gideons. While still in his fifties, the Heinz corporate leadership, knowing his interest and ability in ministry, came to him and offered him full retirement benefits right then, on one condition—

that he would take three months and introduce his younger replacement to all the major accounts in Canada. So Leonard agreed.

One Friday evening, Leonard and his friend were coming back from Nova Scotia and they had to change planes in Montreal. Just as Leonard passed through the gate to enter the awaiting jet that would whisk him home, a French stewardess stopped him without reason and asked Leonard to follow her to board another, slower flight home in an old prop plane.

Here, with baggage already packed, in a hurry to get home, and not wanting to leave his friend, Leonard was more than a little chagrined. But gracious as he was, he obeyed. Only much later did he learn that as that great jet took off, it crashed off the runway, killing everyone aboard.

On the cover of the next morning's *Toronto Daily Star*, Canada's largest newspaper, pictured among the wreckage, was Leonard's Gideon Bible open to this very Scripture: "The Lord hath set apart him that is godly for himself" (Ps. 4:3).

The Canadian Royal Mounted Police grilled Leonard about the incident for days until he finally asked, "Am I under suspicion?" To which they replied, "Anyone who would leave a reserved seat at the last moment like you did must have known something!"

How could a world system know that there is Someone who counts the very hairs on our head? If we give ourselves totally to Him, we have a right to all that He is.

It is the truth of that old Pentecostal song, "Thank God, the doubts are settled, I know it's real!" It's what Paul declared, "I know whom I have believed, and am persuaded that he is able to keep that which I have committed unto him. . ." (2 Tim. 1:12). No churchianity or ritual religion can give those kinds of benefits.

The second great benefit is that true salvation gives meaning, purpose and dignity to life.

I feel especially for today's youths that they are faced with such a vacuum of meaning. They must ask themselves, "Am I the result of mom forgetting to take the pill? Am I just a biological accident? Does anyone really want me or am I just a tax deduction, conceived to prevent the government from getting too much of dad's money?" There is no dignity in this.

Kids today need to know: Who am I? Why am I here? From almost the moment of birth, they are loaned to such a myriad of babysitters that they can hardly recognize their parents. No wonder so many wind up jabbing needles and popping corks in lost bewilderment.

Every child, every person alive, needs to feel valued and important. And this is exactly what we see so vividly in the splendor of the Bible: no two people are born to do the same thing. Every person is distinct and special, with a purpose all his own.

What a beautiful panorama of God's magnificent design and concern. Consider the little fellow in Jesus' day who talked his mother into playing hookey one day to go hear the Master. As an afterthought, the mother packed him a couple of tuna fish sandwiches. Can't you see him running home saying, "Mama, you won't believe this but it will be in all the papers tomorrow—Jesus took my sandwiches and fed five thousand people!"

No other kid in all history has or will have that purpose—to provide the seed food for that explosion of God's bountiful provision.

Then we could move to the other side of the scale and

think of old Simeon, just sitting there in church. You can hear what the saints are saying about him, "He is getting so old, wouldn't it be nice if the Lord would take him home?" What they are really saying is that he is just in the way.

Suddenly, the Lord says to Simeon, "Do you belong to me?"

Simeon replies, "Yes, Lord."

And the Lord says, "Do you see that young couple entering with that baby? He is my only begotten Son! What your eyes have desired to see is here." What a privilege it was to take and hold the living Son of God in his arms and offer the prayer of dedication.

Or we could look at another young person. Here is a twelve-year-old boy coming downstairs at night to say, "There is someone in my room." I used to do the same thing, especially when my parents were having company. I wanted to see who it was, so I'd sneak down with always the same excuse, "I hear someone in my room." I can still hear my Mennonite mother sternly saying, "If you don't get right upstairs, there *will* be someone in your room." We see the Bible is filled with normal people, like you and me.

Well, when Samuel confronted old Eli, Eli recognized who it was. He thought, "He used to come to me, too, but I've grown apostate in my ministry." So Eli told Samuel, "when you hear the voice again, say, 'Speak, Lord, thy servant heareth'." Here is little Samuel tromping up the stairs trying to remember the formula, "Speak, Lord, thy servant heareth; speak, Lord. . . ." That night Almighty God opened the heart of a little twelve-year-old boy and Samuel became the last great judge in Israel.

Every person in the whole Bible has a distinct,

dignified purpose. This is what our youths want and need to hear when on all sides they are being told they're just a statistic, a blob of protoplasm, a number. Society is people—and people will only change when they meet in humble acknowledgement that Great Architect, who has a beautiful, individual plan for every life.

As soon as we do come to pay the true price, to accept God's offer and God's terms, we are on our way to contentment, glory and purpose. Those are benefits worth having.

11

How to Be a Soulwinner

There was an attraction to the person of Jesus that drew crowds wherever He went. This is the greatest quality needed in a soulwinner today to release the presence and attraction of Jesus.

Of the thousands of soul-winning ministries I've seen and heard over the past half century, none would compare with that of Sister Aimee McPherson. Aimee had felt and radiated the compassion of Jesus. Just as our Lord did, she could almost instantly sense the heartbreaks and needs of the people she touched. She never evidenced a doubt concerning God's power to know and meet the need.

Another great soulwinner was the Rev. Paul Rader, founder of Rader Tabernacle in Chicago and pastor of Dwight L. Moody. In contrast to Sister McPherson's touch of compassion, Paul portrayed and proclaimed Jesus to be every ounce a man and every inch a leader. He exhibited all the qualities of a great coach (how like the Holy Spirit) and offered a salvation in Christ that was sure, confident, abundant, and victorious.

Evangelist Billy Sunday, Lance Wilson of the Assemblies, William Booth of the Salvation Army, and Sister Coleman all had strong qualities of the Master that drew millions to Christ. But thankfully today soul-winning is not just the job of the great evangelist or pastor. It is the work of every born-again church member: "He that winneth souls is wise" (Prov. 11:30).

Just as we all know the best fruit is that which is handpicked, the best soul-winning method is personal evangelism. In picking fruit, you don't harvest by shaking the tree and you don't market the windfalls. There is more to soul-winning than organized fervor, shrill publicity and an atmosphere of showmanship.

A conscientious doctor must deal with each patient individually and so must a conscientious soulwinner. The diagnosis is swift in some cases and slow in others—we are to be workmen "that needeth not be ashamed." Can a doctor of souls expect to be less personal or patient than a doctor of bodies? Lives today are fantastically complicated by sin. They need more than slogans and formulas. They need personal help more than professional artistry. Every believer in the congregation is called to be a soulwinner and must be taught the responsibility and privilege that comes with this.

The simplest way to embarrass an ordinary congregation is just to ask two simple questions:

(1) When did you last lead someone to Christ?
(2) When did you last try?

The overwhelming majority are not even trying. Most of us just go on hoping that our lives somehow are exercising a silent influence upon the community. We are tongue-tied. We're willing to pay someone else to tell the story for us.

The task isn't easy—but it's grand. There's no joy like leading a soul to Christ. Everywhere people are in the condition of the parents who came to Christ saying, ". . . Lord, I believe; help thou mine unbelief" (Mark 9:24). People are bound. They live behind an iron curtain of question marks. They haven't really believed anything since they were little children. It's smart to be cynical. People live with their guard up. They expect us to be taken. The skillful personal worker needs to know how to doctor such souls. Otherwise people can pass through a decision line and come away without any real experience of conversion. It's like the devout drunk who had been to a certain mission seven times and thanked God that he had been converted every time.

If only a psychiatrist can lead a soul from darkness to light, then not many folk are going to get saved for there aren't nearly enough psychiatrists to go around. No, my friend, the plain statement of the Master is this: ". . . Come ye after me, and I will make you to become fishers of men" (Mark 1:17). That's what He said, neighbor! Your minister needs your help if your church is going to be an evangelistic church.

You have a personal testimony. What are you doing with it? The obligation to say a good word for Jesus is laid on all Christians. To know Christ and not to pass on the glad news is a criminal negligence. Do you really *know* something? Then tell it. Give your witness for Christ. He is on trial before this world.

"But," you say, "How can I go about it and not offend people?" I suggest these simple rules.

FIRST, LIVE IT.

You can't talk what you don't live. Live it and people will be attracted toward you. They will sense that you have the answer for their need.

SECOND, DON'T TRY TO BE A DO-GOODER— SIMPLY LOVE PEOPLE.

People don't want to be stalked by someone intent on marking up another good deed. A Christian can be radiant with a heaven-sent compassion—an earnestness that simply reaches out after mankind.

THIRD, LEARN TO MEET PEOPLE.

Jesus was heaven's artist at this. He never knew a stranger. Do a kindness toward someone. A kindness will open the door nine times out of ten. Sometimes ask for a favor. Jesus did. He asked the woman at the well for a drink of water. It usually makes people feel good to be asked to help. I don't know why, but it does. When Jesus met Zacchaeus, He did not give him a lecture on the sin of covetousness. He boldly asked himself to lunch.

FOURTH, DISCOVER THE PERSON'S REAL NEED.

An army chaplain put it this way to his men. He would take his watch and say: "Imagine that you have a dying man here. He has two minutes of consciousness before he passes away. Let me hear what you would say in two minutes." Get to the point, neighbor! Don't beat around the bush. Don't be detoured by disguises. Your neighbor is troubled by personal sin. His soul is festering. Behind all his make-believe there is agony and torment. You can help him. You must help him. Get with it. Zacchaeus was in trouble. Uninvited, he babbled about his sin. All his worry and sleepless nights and guilt boiled up in him and he had to tell the things he had kept hidden from the world to this Friend who had invited himself home with him for lunch. You'll be surprised how many people are ready to talk. They simply need someone in whom they can have confidence.

FIFTH, SPEAK NATURALLY.

Your neighbor doesn't understand theological terms or religious phrases. Don't wrap the message in technicalities. They'll learn the proper terms later on when they become children of God. Missionaries learn the language of the natives to whom they go. Soulwinners must learn to speak in a tongue understood by common people.

SIXTH, SPEAK ABOUT CHRIST—NOT ABOUT YOURSELF.

We can get proud about ourselves. I can say, "I was that. I am this. I used to do that. Now I do this." I can get so much "I" into my testimony that spiritual pride will offend the person to whom I am witnessing. The rule of the great Baptist still holds: "He must increase, but I must decrease" (John 3:30). Lift Him up and He will draw all men. Christ is the attraction. Here is the rule: Seven words of Him for every word about yourself. Lift Him up.

SEVENTH, AVOID CONTROVERSY.

Arguments don't make converts. The sinner will gladly find refuge behind the argument, "What church shall I attend?" rather than face the Ten Commandments.

Point out over and over again that the sin problem must be dealt with first. Solving some theological conundrum won't take stealing or lying or hatred out of the human heart. The sinner will know what to do when he gets right with God.

EIGHTH, BRING THEM TO A DECISION.

Decision is not conversion. Decision is an act of the human will. It is a wonderful step. God cannot do His part until man has taken this step. Conversion is what God does. It is the miracle He performs through the ministry of the Holy Spirit. The new birth awaits the moment of personal invitation. "If any man hear my voice, *and open the door,* I will come in to him. . ." (Rev. 3:20, italics mine). The sinner must ask for help.

There is no other way. The latch is on his side of the door. Decision is that grand moment. Postpone it and nothing can happen. Don't be a salesman with a fine presentation of your product and never produce the contract to be signed. So many times a person is won to the point that he is willing or almost willing—but the direct question is not put to him. "Hope deferred maketh the heart sick: but when the desire cometh, it is a tree of life" (Prov. 13:12). So many times the mood passes, and old, perhaps evil, associations rally and woo the sinner away. The chance may never come again. Opportunity is God-given. Don't gamble with it. Press for a decision. "Ye have not because ye ask not." I know that people would be in heaven today if I had had the courage to have asked them to decide for Christ. I hesitated and I was never given another chance.

Every day I live to endeavor to ask God for men and men for God. My fear is my worst enemy. So many people confided in me later that they were waiting to be asked. How many lost souls in eternity will say, "*No Christian ever asked me.*"

NINTH, TEACH THEM TO LISTEN TO GOD'S VOICE.

There is truth in the word, "Acquaint now thyself with him, and be at peace: thereby good shall come unto thee" (Job 22:21). So many personal workers acquaint the seeker only with himself or herself. That is a major mistake. Your business is to lead that soul to God. Let that soul hear for the first time the voice of God speaking to him in reassurance and comfort—and you have built strength. Otherwise that soul is no stronger than the arm of flesh upon which it is leaning. You say, "Brother Ward, how can I teach the soul I wish to lead to Christ to listen to God's voice?" How? By teaching that person two or three primary verses of Scripture. Tie the seeker to God's Word. Let your friend know before you leave him that God has spoken these words to him. These divine words carry a guaranteed promise. Here is an example: ". . . He that heareth my word, and believeth on him that sent me, hath everlasting life, and shall not come into condemnation; but is passed from death unto life" (John 5:24). That's a big statement. It covers a lot of ground. But who said it? Jesus Christ. If those were simply my words they would be wonderful but purely sentimental and wishful thinking. They might be poetical but at the same time they would be quite powerless. But they are His words. Therein lies the difference.

In leading a soul to Christ I must teach that man or woman at once that there is a difference between knowing about God and knowing God himself. You know Him through His Word. Without this they will miss their way. The devil will deceive them before breakfast. He will lie to them so cleverly that they will apologize to their worldly associates before the day is over for making fools of themselves at the evangelistic service the night before.

Always remember it, personal worker, your word is not enough. Teach the one you are dealing with to listen to God's voice. That's where Christian strength begins. When you think of all the matted problems of people's lives and the festering disquietude within them and then remember that for every one of them there is a cure in Christ, there comes a longing to get them to Him.

> Rescue the perishing, Care for the dying,
> Snatch them in pity from sin and the grave;
> Weep o'er the erring one, Lift up the fallen,
> Tell them of Jesus, the mighty to save.

Down in the human heart, Crushed by the
    tempter
Feelings lie buried that grace can restore;
Touched by a loving heart, Wakened by
    kindness,
Chords that are broken will vibrate once
    more.

(Fanny J. Crosby)

    Those words are just as true today as the day Fanny Crosby wrote them. People need help. The sin-stained and inferior, the proud and the resentful, the sex-obsessed and sex-perverted, the prayerless and chronically selfish, the divorced and those planning divorces, the lonely, the unbelieving, the disillusioned and the delinquent, sick souls every one of them, and they all need help.

    Wouldn't you like to see one soul made whole again? Wouldn't you like to stand by and say, "That person was sick, broken and lost, but now he is whole again. I'm glad it was in my power to lead him to Christ." Wouldn't you like that thrill? Then let me tell you, Christian friend, "This is not a preacher's monopoly. You can do it too." God will help any individual who wants to do it. God will send His Spirit upon you for such service. The Master waits to say the same words to you as He once said to Peter, ". . . Fear not; from henceforth thou shalt catch men" (Luke 5:10).

12

Tongues of Fire

The Bible is pretty clear in saying that what is important is not how much you get but how you use what you get. And that, it seems, was our problem early in our denomination with the Holy Spirit. We were more concerned with people getting the Holy Spirit than teaching them how to use the Spirit (or to be used of Him).

We took courses in Bible school on how to lead people into the fullness of the Holy Spirit. Then we spent many years in the pastorate trying gently to corral and control the wildfire brought on by the people receiving the baptism of the Spirit and tongues.

The Bible explains why this happened. *Tongues are the New Testament circumcision.*

In the Old Testament, God placed a physical mark upon His called ones, His witnesses. This was a "branding." The mark could not be erased. It spoke of ownership and purpose.

God would do no less with His New Testament 'Israel,' His *ecclesia*. Fifty days after the blood was applied in Egypt, Israel came to Mt. Sinai. There Israel embraced a contract. Likewise, fifty days after Christ offered himself as the Passover, the believer came to Mt. Zion. A new contract was in force. There were lightnings and thunder at Sinai. Similarly at Zion, "suddenly there came a sound from heaven. . . . there appeared unto them cloven tongues like as of fire" (Acts 2:2-3).

In the Old Testament, the mark was placed upon an exceedingly mischievous member of the body. Likewise, in the New Testament: "And the tongue is a fire, a world of iniquity: So is the tongue among our members, that it defileth the whole body, and setteth on fire the course of nature; and, it is set on fire of hell. . . . But the tongue can no man tame" (James 3:6-10).

But when heaven sets it on fire, you have the results Peter knew in his message to Jerusalem. How different to the shame and loss he experienced in the courtyard! "Then began he to curse and to swear, saying, I know not the man" (Matt. 26:74).

When God "kindles" the tongue there is a witness that changes lives.

Zephaniah saw it prophetically: "For then will I turn to the people a *pure language,* that they may all call upon the name of the Lord" (Zeph. 3:9 italics mine).

Heaven supernaturally divided language—"confound their language, that they may not understand one another's speech" (Gen. 11:7)—and even so, heaven will supernaturally teach mankind a "pure language."

The purpose is *evangelism,* that, "the knowledge of the Lord [shall cover the earth] as the waters cover the sea" (Isa. 11:9).

Every language on this planet has been sullied, engaged to promote filth, vulgarity, obscenity.

God intends *a new language* for the "new heavens and a new earth."

Thus, the utterance of a believer promises a future day free from innuendo, uncleanness, "filthy communication."

Glossalalia is a forecast of a better society.

Tongues also speak of Calvary.

Years ago, I traveled to Huntsville, Alabama, and Redstone Arsenal to interview the great space scientist, Dr. Wernher von Braun.

He spoke to me about the waning days of Hitler when von Braun was commanding a research base on the Baltic. The great scientist said that as the end approached, he called a prayer meeting among his colleagues.

He paused and directed this remark to me, "Brother Ward," he said, "you may find it incredible to believe God understands *German*. But let me tell you something," he said, "God not only *understands* German, He speaks it *fluently*."

As with a heavenly thud, in that great man's office, I was struck by the truth, *Calvary is for everybody*. God so loves the French, the Mexican, the Chinese, the Russian—everyone. Calvary is not for English-speaking people only.

Tongues tells me that!

There are, however, two parts to tongues and all spiritual gifts—the human and the divine. These are divine gifts but they operate through human channels. God's part is 100% supernatural but man's part is natural—subject to error and mistake. If prophecy and tongues and interpretation were 100% supernatural, they would be infallible and could not be judged. But God's Word says, "Let the prophets speak two or three, and let the other judge" (1 Cor. 14:29).

God recognizes the "human element" involved and commands that these gifts be judged. Much of the controversy today over the gift of tongues involves its use (and/or misuse) in public gatherings of worship. There is still much misunderstanding although the Bible gives clear direction for the use of this gift.

The first misunderstanding is *where* the gift should be used. There is a private use of tongues for personal edification. But in public, the gifts of inspiration (including tongues) are given exclusively for the edification of the church—that company of believers filled with the Holy Ghost. Tongues have no mention or purpose in an evangelistic service.

The use of this gift is by faith. Some think that one must be physically "moved on" by the Spirit. Paul warns that the gifts may be neglected, so we should "stir up the gift" that is within—we should exercise it.

We can and ought to control the gift of tongues: "the spirits of the prophets are subject to the prophets." The Lord has placed upon us the responsibility for the due restraint as well as the due operation of the gift. Paul gives us clear guidelines: First, though all can speak at once in other tongues, we shouldn't. Second, there should be two, or at most three, messages in tongues and each must be interpreted. If there is no interpretation, the gift must be withheld (see 1 Cor. 14:27-28).

The confusion over the gift of tongues arises not from God but rather from man's neglect of God's Word. But the encouragement to the church is that only where there is life is there danger of disorder. Paul says, "Forbid not to speak with tongues" (1 Cor. 14:39). In other words, it is much better to learn (even with mistakes) to use the gift properly than to prohibit its use.

The final test of proper employment of this gift is always edification. "Let all things be done unto edifying" (1 Cor. 14:26).

One of my worst experiences in this area happened in

Melbourne, Australia. I had scarcely begun to preach my message in this large hall when a man stood and gave me both barrels in tongues and the interpretation. The essence of his lengthy tirade was, "Yankee, go home!" Now, anywhere in the world you will experience a measure of anti-Americanism, and Australians are rather independent. But this was cruel and pathetic.

I listened patiently and then spoke out, "You may or may not have noticed but I didn't close my eyes during your message. You were quite busy. But as the Bible says, my mission was to judge. And I was busy judging that message. In my judgment, it was rotten. *Rotten!"*

I continued, "For your information, sir, unless my hosts decide otherwise, I am not going to leave this nation one second before I am scheduled to do so. Now be my guest. You have declared your heart and I have listened. If you will give me the same courtesy to declare myself while you listen, I would be most happy. Otherwise, we'll wait until you leave."

My mouth spoke strongly but inside I was devastated that someone would use this medium to release venom. But then I remembered how Satan tempted Jesus. He will imitate God's best.

Sometimes, the timing or the attitude is the problem and not the message. One summer during the Korean conflict, I was invited to be the speaker at a large Methodist campground meeting in Cumberland, Maryland. A great percentage of the audience were denominational people, so I was preaching a simple message geared to salvation.

Just as I was about to give the altar call, a rather stoutly built woman stood and gave out a blast in tongues. At the time, I was unsure of whether this was of the flesh or of God. The Bible says to "try the spirits," so I asked God for discernment.

I remembered that Paul says that the heavenly tongue is a sign to the unbeliever. So it could be an asset in closing this meeting to bring people to the altar. With that in mind, I said, "I thank God and heaven for additional choir power and help. Now if our sister will just come with that intercessory spirit to this altar and pour her heart out there, it will be the very touch God wants for this service."

In that moment, she showed her true self. She was in the flesh and started another blast—because she wanted to perform rather than to minister.

That is always the way of the flesh—to glamorize. This is the business of Hollywood, Broadway and Madison Avenue. This is the way industry promotes and sells everything from breakfast foods to cosmetics. Glamour is an outside effort, hopefully working toward the inside.

The ministry of the Holy Spirit, however, is to *glorify*—Jesus. Jesus said, "He shall glorify me" (John 16:14). Glory is not a fourth-of-July psychedelic experience, but an *inside* experience that changes the outside. "[He] was transfigured before them: and his face did shine as the sun, and his raiment was white as the light" (Matt. 17:2).

When her intention became evident, I found it necessary to teach her a lesson in order to protect the gathering. So I asked an associate to maintain the music of the moment while I went down into the audience. Passing by her husband—I hooked my arm under this lady's arm and said, "I have asked you kindly to come. And under God I am in charge of running this meeting. Now I want you at that altar—not standing here drawing attention. I want you to draw attention to Jesus—because that is why the Holy Spirit is given to us."

With that, I pulled her out from that seat and marched her down the aisle and put her at the altar. To my surprise, she came back the next night, showing she was just a babe in these things and needed instruction and good handling. With a small amount of further admonishment, she behaved herself well.

Pastor Lewi Pethrus of Stockholm, Sweden, was perhaps the best I ever saw when it comes to exercising pastoral authority in this area. I was his pulpit guest for a Good Friday communion service, with the auditorium at capacity. Suddenly, a well-meaning sister began an utterance. Without hesitation Pastor Pethrus said, "Not now, sister!"

The lady was not offended. She was simply obedient. The congregation respected the pastor's proven leadership. Later in the service Pastor Pethrus turned to the same member and said, "Now, sister!" She obeyed quickly and all were blessed.

It is vital, therefore, for a pastor to have and to exercise the gift of discernment. Under God, this prevents the misuse of the spiritual gifts from snarling the flow of God. People are always hungry to be in that God-given flow. A church that has it is guaranteed to grow.

Photo Section

Young C.M.—the year after his marriage to Dorothy (1930).

Dorothy—"Whoso findeth a wife findeth a good thing" (Prov. 18:22).

Both Dorothy (left) and her sister, Esther-Deane, were talented singers. Here we are with Esther-Deane's boy friend, Leonard Palmer, in front of the Hymes home in Ottawa, Kansas.

Bud Van Der Plog, Dorothy and I often worked together as an evangelistic team in the early '40s.

See, pastoral calls can be fun after all. I'm still smiling, today!

In 1940, Tommy Hadingswood (left), Richard Penley (center) and brother Emmett (right) joined our musical family for Jesus.

C.M., Dorothy and Martha Jane, while pastoring in Bakersfield (1946).

Photo Section

Grandpa Ward with Shalanne (1974).

Dr. and Mrs. C.M. Ward—Golden Wedding anniversary (1929-1979).

C.M. cuts a cake to celebrate with Jim and Tammy Bakker on "The PTL Club."

C.M. and Dorothy at Bethany.

Dr. C.M. Ward (1979).

13

Preaching and Boo-Boos

A primary task of every pastor is to preach.

Without reservation I believe the truth of 1 Corinthians 1:21, "It pleased God by the foolishness of *preaching* to *save.*"

There can be no satisfactory substitute for preaching, although countless attempts have been made. Always, it seems, this dynamic medium is under attack.

Many question the charismatic movement. They raise this issue: "How much of the 'spirit' is due to movements of the Holy Spirit, and how much is due to the *mere soul-movements* of men?"

They want to credit personal magnetism, positive thinking, emotional techniques—anything—rather than to admit to the supernatural. "But unto them which are called, ... Christ the power of God, and the wisdom of God" (1 Cor. 1:24).

Professional training sometimes attempts to implant these doubts within candidates for the ministry. The *caution* to suppress every feeling, is to make religion a cold, ethical treatment, not much different from a refined, pagan philosophy.

Why this strident barrage to remove all heat and energy from the pulpit and give us pablum? Why do these "fuddy-duddies" seek to minimize the power of

God in the pulpit? Why do they want to explain the Wesley, Finney, Moody and Sunday eras as "psychological movements"? Why do they want to ascribe results to *men* and not to *God?*

Such people are deceived by "seducing spirits" (1 Tim. 4:1).

They would substitute a ministry which hesitates to *proclaim* for fear that peers will judge them as being unintellectual. The result is that the pulpit produces a weak and hesitant testimony instead of a "thus saith the Lord." And much of the time there is neither soul-power nor God-power.

No one questioned Paul's academic credentials. He was not restrained by any fear of hypnotic effect upon his hearers. He was alive, passionate, full of what the Bible calls the power of the Holy Spirit.

So vehement was he that Festus trembled, while Agrippa thought that Paul's learning had made him mad.

Our politicians today need to hear that kind of preaching.

No investigator could possibly ascribe the effect of Paul's preaching to an overwhelming Hollywood or Madison Avenue image. He came in "weakness," and he was the first to admit his infirmities. *He was never a physical attraction.* With Paul, it was clearly the power of God.

A dead message cannot bring results. And a live message from a dead preacher is an impossibility. It is so difficult for these "wise ones" to ever understand that "the letter. . . *killeth*," no matter how brilliantly taught, with the best academic, doctrinal treatment. It is "the Spirit that *quickeneth.*"

The gospel of the Son of God is the "power of God" (Rom. 1:16).

No seminary can produce the magic formula, the "party communique," the proper service, the "acceptable." It is not in rhetoric, oratory, debate, skillful presentation. It is, as Paul declares, "For the kingdom of God is not in *word*, but in *power*" (1 Cor. 4:20). It is not in mesmerism, hypnotism, or in any of the psychological forces. It is in *power*.

Matthew 11:20-23 uses the same root meaning as "mighty works." There is nothing *negative* about it. This power—"the strength of the Divine"—which clothes the preacher is *aggressive*, a mighty force taking hold, turning from evil to good, making new men and women. It is not a natural thing. *It is supernatural.*

How shall a man know, then, what is the power of the Holy Spirit, and that which is merely human?

There is only one way of knowing—the old test suggested by Jesus—"by their fruits."

Whatever movement issues in regenerated lives, whatever makes evil men good, that is the power of the Holy Spirit. It is not in man to make himself good, or work transformation in another man; no suggestion, no clinical psychological treatment, *no human power*—possessed by the strongest among men—*can change a sinful man into a godly man.*

"Do men gather grapes of thorns, or figs of thistles? Even so every good tree bringeth forth good fruit; but a corrupt tree bringeth forth evil fruit. A good tree cannot bring forth evil fruit, neither can a corrupt tree bring forth good fruit" (Matt. 7:16-18).

So my advice to any preacher is to "let go and let God." This byline was acceptable to heaven: "The sword of the Lord, and of Gideon" (Judg. 7:18). God means for the blend, the intermingling, to be so perfect that it is more than difficult to know where the one stops and the other begins.

I come to the pulpit conscious that Another over-shadows me, that the Greater Hand covers mine, that the Eternal uses my voice and faculties. Without such an anointing I would not want to preach.

In the pulpit and in all of life, expectancy is an important key to victory. "For as he *thinketh* in his heart, so is he" (Prov. 23:7, italics mine); the word "thinketh" could properly be translated "expecteth." It is not as much what you believe or desire or think as what you expect that counts. A conviction goes deeper than a thought, just as an intuition does. What we are convinced of, we expect. It is already headed our way.

No matter how proper and eloquent I could make my words, without that expectancy that God would take those words and transform them into life and power in the hearers, I could not face any congregation—no matter how much the pay.

Sometimes, our Bible schools can put such emphasis on proper techniques and methods that both the human conviction and the divine anointing are lost. So often, rather, God chooses the weak and foolish—"that no flesh should glory in his presence" (1 Cor. 1:29). God must loose us, as preachers, to let His Spirit flow—as well as to let our humanness show.

Early in my ministry, I dramatically discovered that God sometimes uses preachers not because of their abilities but in spite of them. It happened in one of the first conventions where I was invited to be the featured speaker.

In the middle of my message, I was making an important point. To dramatize it to my audience, I went to sit down on the folding chair by the podium. I forgot that the platform wasn't carpeted and the chair went flying back as I sat, sending me sprawling on my back.

My descent must have been a thing of beauty. The audience thought I had been slain in the Spirit and entered into spontaneous praise. It brought God's Spirit into the entire convention and produced a mighty spirit of revival and faith unlike anything that church had ever experienced.

After that, I worried less about preaching techniques and concerned myself more with being sensitive to the Spirit. I let Dorothy be my worrier about outward appearances. She did help me a lot in that area when she finally sewed up all my pants pockets, so I couldn't constantly put my hands in and out of them.

Over the years, I have had the "pleasure" of seeing many of my colleagues exhibit a touch of humanness, too. One morning we had a visiting speaker who was married to a talented violinist. Before his sermon, he made this announcement: "And now, Mr—will come up and fiddle with my wife."

On another occasion, when I was working at general headquarters, a very prestigious member of the ladies auxiliary was chosen to address a convention. Her opening line was this: "While I was sitting on my mind this thought shot through my seat." It broke up the whole convention.

I've had my share of boo-boos too, though nothing quite so spectacular. It is just one of many fears a preacher faces and must learn to overcome. One of my greatest fears in later years was that I might develop the urgency to sneeze when I would do radio sermons. The enemy would tantalize me with the thought, "You're going to sneeze and the whole network will laugh at you."

Learning to be human and laugh at yourself quenches a lot of the enemy darts and again frees one to "let go and let God." A pastor who is free to be himself and who will receive the burden of the Holy Spirit will never lack for a message to preach.

14

Pastoring

One of the most important things any pastor must learn is who he is—before both God and his fellowman. That's because a pastor can be so many things to so many people.

He can be an administrator in the church; he can be the janitor. He can be the resident psychiatrist; he can be under constant analysis by his people. He can be the loudspeaker; he can be the earplug. He can be the doctor; he can be the peacemaker.

All these functions may be part of the pastor's duties, but they are not his chief calling.

We have one true and perfect example of pastoral leadership—Jesus Christ. "Our Lord Jesus, that great shepherd of the sheep. . ." (Heb. 13:20).

It was no accident that Jesus, himself, likened His leadership of the Church to that of a shepherd to his sheep.

Flocks of sheep dotted the countryside of Palestine in Jesus' day. The work of the shepherd was an ancient profession, with well-recognized standards and duties. The shepherd always went ahead of his sheep, leading them—never driving them. He had a special call with which he summoned his own flock. His sheep would answer that call and no other.

In cool weather, he led the sheep to pasture from the morning until evening. In warm weather, he took them to the fold for safety while he took his own rest. The fold was enclosed to protect the sheep from harsh weather and fenced to keep out intruders. A guard received the sheep into the fold as the shepherds called for them.

Therefore, when Christ revealed that He was the Great Shepherd of the Church, the flock of God, His hearers understood this perfectly. He added that all who answer His call are united into one flock under one Shepherd.

But Jesus carefully trained and commissioned His disciples to be "pastors," or undershepherds of the flock, to carry on and extend His Word, under His leadership as Chief Pastor. Therefore, the mandate of pastors is clearly laid out: they are to lead, protect, and feed the sheep and to keep them from being scattered—and above all to guide and protect God's people so they can be fed and nourished.

So pastors must be careful not to major in minors. More than once, God has had to bring me back to center stage and remind me of His calling.

On one occasion I tried to play chief psychologist at the Minister's Institute in Louisiana. This is a big event that is always held in West Monroe. They have one of the greatest choirs in all the South and the people come to hear the music as much as the speaker.

I was again invited to be the guest speaker. After the performance by the choir, I was announced and presented to this huge, overflow crowd. But before I was to give the message, I was to turn the platform over to a young musician, Larry, who would minister by accompanying the choir.

Instead of just doing as I was told, I perceived that the choir and its director could use a little encouragement.

So with my best eloquence and at the expense of Larry (of whom I had no knowledge), I said, "Larry is probably least needed here." I could hear a titter behind my back and the gasping of the choir members. The more I praised the present choir and leadership and diminished the need of Larry, the deeper the hole I dug for myself grew. I could see it but didn't understand it.

When the laughter subsided at my expense, and I finally welcomed Larry onto the stage, he turned out to be the son of the district superintendent, my host. My big attempt at being psychologist turned into one of the bigger boners of my life.

That was one time I put my head into something I should have stayed out of. Other times, I had to learn, as a shepherd, to put my head into things that I would have rather avoided. One of these was dealing with my church board.

A congregation should not be afraid of its pastor and a pastor must never be afraid of his people or his board. Learning to stand up to the board is something that comes by experience and the anointing of the Spirit.

In one pastorate, I got wind, at the last moment, that a board meeting was being held in the church treasurer's home without me. The Holy Spirit impressed me to go and check it out. I arrived just as they were getting down to business. Talk about a startled group of men!

Finally, the instigator mumbled, "Pastor, we weren't doing anything behind your back. We just knew how busy you were and we thought it would help if we took care of some details."

Without sitting down, I addressed them, "Gentlemen, I take this as being tantamount to a vote of lack of confidence. And I suggest that you are not behaving as men. If you feel unanimously that I have reached the close of my ministry here, call me in. Otherwise, we have a constitution and bylaws which dictate that I am chairman of this board. I didn't call this meeting, did I?"

A sheepish voice answered, "No, pastor, you didn't."

"Then it's out of order," I replied. "Finish your cup of coffee and leave. The meeting's dismissed."

In another pastorate, I had some enthusiastic young board members, who added a lot of effort, but they did not always exhibit wisdom. On one occasion, these young bucks were determined to ramrod an idea through whether I or the rest of the board liked it or not. They were well-prepared for a head-on confrontation with me.

Just before things got to a head, I rose and said, "Men, it's getting rather late and I need my rest. So I am going home."

When I did, one of the antagonists said, "But—but— pastor, that's not the way it's done. You can't do this."

I said, "You will now see the way it's done. Nothing productive is being accomplished right now and life is too short to be spent quibbling and quarreling. So if you'll excuse me, I'm leaving."

Next morning, one of the board members called and said, "C.M., we didn't stay long after you left but we did realize that we are not as close to you as we'd like to be. We would like you and your wife to be our guests for dinner at the finest restaurant in the county."

I said, "That is a really fine decision. Yes, very good!"

In the years that I pastored, I guess nearly every one of my board members resigned at least once. But in each case, I went to his home within twenty-four hours and said, "I don't think you'll be happy with your resignation. I know I'm not happy with it. I love you and I know you basically love me. You need my ministry and I certainly need your counsel and advice. So come on back." They all came back.

I recently read a good article by a pastor who said that what many churches need is some good creative disagreement. I agree—controversy speaks of movement and life. The important ingredient in controversy, whether in the pulpit or in business, concerns how you deal with it.

Unfortunately, most pastors deal with the negative defensively, by throwing back negatives. One doesn't fight disease with disease. Disease must be fought with health. When faced with criticism or conflict, positive action is absolutely necessary. Without this, Satan will come and paralyze.

A person will be useless, incompatible, and unemployable as long as he or she curdles and gives place to a "root of bitterness." There is not much of a market for bitter people. They are like rancid meat.

Naomi was a bitter person when she returned from Moab with her daughter-in-law, Ruth. Both were widows. Both had sustained loss. One chose to look on the sunny side. The other chose to look on the dark side.

Naomi's frame of mind paralyzed her: "Call me not Naomi, call me Mara: for the Almighty hath dealt very bitterly with me. I went out full, and the Lord hath brought me home again empty: why then call ye me Naomi, seeing the Lord hath testified against me, and the Almighty hath afflicted me" (Ruth 1:20, 21).

Grief is one thing. But above that Naomi suffered from a bruised ego. That is a virus that ruins one's usefulness. The vaccine is the remedy Jesus proposes: "Love your enemies, bless them that curse you, do good to them that hate you, and pray for them which despitefully use you, and persecute you; That ye may be the children of your Father which is in heaven" (Matt. 5:44-45).

"And why beholdest thou the mote that is in thy brother's eye, but considerest not the beam that is in thine own eye? Or how wilt thou say to thy brother, Let me pull out the mote out of thine eye; and behold, a beam is in thine own eye? Thou hypocrite, first cast out the beam out of thine own eye; and then shalt thou see clearly to cast out the mote out of thy brother's eye" (Matt. 7:3-5).

My mother taught me these lines which have often been my guidance:

> "There is so much good in the worst of us,
> And so much bad in the best of us;
> That it ill behooves any of us,
> To be hard on the rest of us."

So often when we judge and cancel out another, we only result in condemning ourselves. The old kid's adage is true, "It takes one to know one." More often than not, our judgment reveals more about ourselves than the person we're judging: "For thou that judgest doest the same things" (Rom. 2:1).

Early in my pastoral life, I learned to check my spirit when faced with conflict and criticism. I would ask myself, "Am I in any way reacting defensively? Am I giving any place for the enemy to enter into my ego? What positive action can I take to love and help that person who is confronting me negatively?"

Whether it was dealing with my people, the board or my staff, I was always in there to win. Basically, not because I had to win for myself, but because I knew the place where God had put me—"we are more than conquerors."

Billy Graham once startled his listeners at a crusade when he boldly declared, "A Christian who is not living victoriously is really a freak." When God created man, He declared, "let them *have dominion*" (Gen. 1:26). In Revelation, Jesus' promises of heavenly reward were "to him that overcometh will I give. . ." (Rev. 2:7).

To quote General McArthur, "There can be no substitute for victory." A believer will either live in victory or he will stagnate. The pastor, therefore, in every service, in his every contact with his people, should demand and effect results to bring that divine "self-sacrificing love" to his flock.

15

The Leader

When you're young they call it brashness. When you're older, they call it wise leadership. Whatever it is, as shepherd of the flock, a pastor needs lots of it.

To board members and parishioners alike, I'm sure I often appeared more than a little brash. But I never apologized for it. Pastoral authority must come from God: "There was a man *sent* from God, whose name was John" (John 1:6).

Anything less than a divine assignment in the pulpit reduces the office to contemptible politics, groveling employment, crawling subservience and lack of self-esteem.

In one of my first pastorates in Canada, the church was large and I was trying to motivate the people to build the congregation, without much success. So I first met with the church board and then all the members. I said to them, "How many seats in the auditorium do you wish to have filled? I do not want to admire or preach to furniture. I can do that at a furniture store. You all decide and then we will get rid of all the extra seats before next Sunday."

Then I added, "If you decide to keep all the seats, then decide which way you want them filled. You can do the job yourself and bring the people in or you can have me go out into the highways and hedges to do the job. If the latter is your sovereign decision, do not criticize me for establishing a flow of traffic. I am simply about my Father's business. And, remember, I gave you first choice."

It may have been brash but this straightforward talk worked like magic. Pretty soon the church was filled and the people weren't letting me do it all by myself, either.

This did another marvelous thing: it established my pastoral authority right from the start. And when that question is resolved, it makes it easy for the love affair between pulpit and pew to build. God, himself, is the matchmaker.

As a pastor or leader, you will be what you *expect* to be. So set your ideals high! "Set your affection on things above, not on things on the earth" (Col. 3:2). Don't grovel!

I have always told superintendents, "The best way to be a successful superintendent is to accept and enjoy all the advantages the office provides. The heartaches will take care of themselves."

There is nothing worse than a *patronizing* attitude. When I am the guest of black congregations, I open with this: "The only black person I can't respect is the black who is ashamed to be black. I expect you to be as proud to be black as a Boston Irishman is to be Irish. If you feel it is your life's mission to be sorry, be sorry for me. I don't know who arranged the piano keyboard, but I know that whoever did, didn't place all the black keys on one end and all the white keys on the other end. We are going to have to respect and appreciate each other to execute harmony and music." That usually gets the job done.

Taking strong leadership doesn't make an easy road for the pastor. For then the people really do look to you for guidance. Many times I've been unsure of my leadership. I have sought God and still have not been sure.

After fifty years of experience, this is what I've discovered works best for me: *Desperation is always better than despair.*

I lean on this scriptural support:

> And there were four leprous men at the entering in of the gate: and they said one to another, Why sit we here until we die? If we say, We will enter into the city, then the famine is in the city, and we shall die there: and if we sit still here, we die also. *Now therefore come,* and let us fall unto the host of the Syrians: *if they save us alive, we shall live; and if they kill us, we shall but die.*
>
> And they rose up in the twilight, to go unto the camp of the Syrians: and when they were come to the uttermost part of the camp of Syria, behold, there was no man there.
>
> For the Lord had made the host of the Syrians to hear a noise of chariots, and a noise of horses, even the noise of a great host: and they said one to another, Lo, the king of Israel hath hired against us the kings of the Hittites, and the kings of the Egyptians, to come upon us.
>
> Wherefore they arose and fled in the twilight. . . . And when these lepers came to the uttermost part of the camp, they went into one tent, and did eat and drink. . . . (2 Kings 7:3-9)

General Stonewall Jackson of the Confederacy ran his brigade successfully on *two basic commands:*

Keep your ranks closed, and *keep moving.*
Jesus noted and commended the woman who "kept moving":

> And, behold, a woman, which was diseased with an issue of blood twelve years, came behind him, and touched the hem of his garment: For she said within herself. . . .

She was not willing to give up and die—though the experts gave her no encouragement:

> Which had spent all her living upon physicians, neither could be healed of any. (Luke 9:20, 21)

I have found that some of the greatest inspiration is borne out of desperation. At least, it has been that way in my life.

In one instance, I had been invited down to Haiti to do a crusade. The little hall (hardly more than a hut) in which we were meeting was packed and overflowing. As I began to get into the heart of my message, a little baby, no doubt hungry, began bawling and squalling. The competition was way too strong to even try to continue preaching.

In desperation, I stopped my message and spoke to the mother, saying, "Has that baby been baptized or dedicated to the Lord?"

She looked at me kind of funny. "No, Reverend," she replied.

"Oh, well, that is the problem then," I said. And motioned for the mother to bring the howling child to me. As I took the baby and prayed, the little thing drifted right off to sleep. From then on, that congregation drank in my every word. They all wanted me to pray for them.

If you are seeking God, doing *something* will always be better than doing *nothing*.

One of my favorite people is Mr. Ray Kroc, President of McDonald's Hamburger chain and crusty owner of the San Diego Padres—the man who lost his temper and won a town.

Kroc says, "If you can't sell the steak, sell the sizzle."

And nothing is as tasteless as lack of effort and determination.

One day soon after having purchased this professional baseball club, Kroc observed the sloppy, listless play of the team. In anger, he commandeered the press box microphone and apologized to the crowd, calling the players a bunch of hamburgers.

Needless to say, the fervency of the team picked up remarkably.

Billy Sunday had that kind of fervency and it inspired all of us who heard him. It was in his heart and it flowed out 100% of the time.

An Iowa farmer's description of Billy says it all:

> See here, Jones; there never was any preachin' done jes like that baseball man does it. I tell you, John, he's got more life in him than any two-year-old colt you ever saw. I would never 'a' believed it if I hadn't seen it, that anybody would ever be so much in airnest at jes' preachin'.
>
> He's got a platform to stand on more'n as big as two wagon boxes, and he kivers every inch of it in every sermon he preaches. Why, in the meetin' last Sunday he got so fired up that he

tore off his tie with his vest and coat, and even rolled up his sleeves as if he was a-goin' to help thrash.

My, how he does wake folks up, an' keep 'em on tenderhooks! Go to sleep? Well, I should say not! Not under the preachin' that's done in that tent. Why, John, he pounds his point clear through you, and makes 'em stick out on the other side. I thought I'd been ahearin' ruther strong preachin' all my life, but I never heard non that took hold of me like his'n does.

The baptism of the Holy Spirit is a baptism of fire and enthusiasm. Church leadership should be filled with it from the preacher to the song leader down to the ushers.

"For our God is a consuming fire" (Heb. 12:29).

Such a God will never tolerate lackadaisical leadership. Never!

16

Heroes

This is the age of superheroes. But the only superheroes I know are in the comic strips or on TV or in the movies. God has given all of us a heart of flesh.

Young preachers and students chuckle when I say that I go AWOL every day at about four o'clock in the afternoon. But I am comforted to know the biggest names in the ministry have done the same—Elijah, Jonah, Peter, Mark and others.

Standing tall doesn't mean you never become afraid. Someone once said, "The only difference between a hero and a coward is that the hero hangs in there for five minutes longer." This is largely true.

The devil will always offer man a way out. When Jesus hungered in the wilderness seeking God's will, the devil tempted him to settle for the earthly satisfaction of bread. Similarly, Satan tries to make the temporal treasures of earth better to man than the eternal heavenly treasures.

To Job, Satan offered the way out to "Curse God, and die" (Job 2:9). That is the ultimate trap and lie. The Bible says, "There hath no temptation taken you but such as is common to man: but God is faithful who will not suffer you to be tempted above that ye are able; but will with the temptation also make a way to escape, that ye may be able to bear it" (1 Cor. 10:13). Obedience to God's will is the only true way of escape.

Preachers must face more than their share of fear. It isn't easy to stand behind "home plate" (the pulpit) and call right or wrong with the rule book in your hands. And it is never popular. Satan will tempt every minister to speak what the congregation wants to hear rather than what they ought to hear or what God wants to say.

If you must choose in life, it is better to be respected than to be loved. Few baseball umpires are loved but they are respected. Paul put it on the line to the believers in Corinth: "Now I pray to God that ye do no evil; not that we should appear approved, but that ye should do that which is honest, though we be as reprobates" (2 Cor. 13:7).

If you let the reactions of people determine your actions, you are doomed for sure. Most every church is full of Monday morning "armchair quarterbacks." Whether you are the preacher or a lay worker, you'll find there are hundreds who can tell you how to get the job done. But few of them are doing it themselves. James tells us, "But be ye doers of the word, and not hearers only, deceiving your own selves. For if any be a hearer of the word, and not a doer, he is like unto a man beholding his natural face in a glass: For he beholdeth himself and goeth his way, and straightway forgetteth what manner of man he was" (James 1:22-24).

James goes on to say that it is by our *acts* of kindness that we are blessed.

My father, Elder A.G. Ward, had a favorite line, "Aim to be a felt necessity." What he meant is that each of us is a separate, distinct package. As such, we are marketable items. In the world, there are enough people who will find in us, not only compatibility, but attraction. So, we must stand our ground and offer the "gift" God has given us to share with humanity.

There is a difference between fear and what the British have called *funk* (cowardice). Fear is a normal instinct. Without it, recklessness, presumption and insanity will prevail. Fear keeps me from getting run over. Fear teaches me to dress and eat sensibly.

It is the cowardly thing that I must face and conquer at all times.

Every time I step up to the pulpit, it's another service. And I must conquer those butterflies about the unknown. My thoughts run wild: Do I have the message of God? What will be the reaction of the congregation? Will there be results or disappointment? It's thump after thump. I groan, "If it be possible let this . . . pass." It saps my energy as I step before the people so alone.

But, oh, there is victory ahead!

There is always victory when we face our fears in Christ. "Greater is he that is in you, than he that is in the world" (1 John 4:4).

There are many confrontations in life and they must be faced. You will never be free until you face them. Esther concluded, "And if I perish, I perish" (Esth. 4:16). Shakespeare observes, "Cowards die many times before their deaths; the valiant never taste of death but once."

The enemy would try to tempt us not to face those needed confrontations. He whispers, "You might fail, you might be disgraced or disappointed. Let it be and it may go away." It is fear of failure that produces cowards.

Our God, who is with us, has never failed! And He will not fail nor forsake us. In Christ, we can not lose when we bring Him to bear on our confrontations.

Perhaps the greatest eternal value of the sports we learned as kids is that they teach us this lesson: Every baseball player who steps into a batter's box knows about confrontation. To face a ball traveling ninety miles an hour from sixty feet away, takes strong resolve and desire to hang in there and not bail out. That urge to hit the ball a mile can push back cowardice till it has no effect.

It is the same with auto racing. Dick Mittman, the great reporter, says, "The drivers have told me that you have to have *respect* for speed, but you can't have fear. Once you are ever afraid, you might as well quit because you lose your confidence."

Facing the fears in life breeds confidence. That is the "vitamin C" the inner man needs every day. God is always saying to me, *"It is I, be not afraid!"*

God has enabled us to live in victory. But we must daily say to our souls, "I will fear no evil: for thou *art* [present tense] with me" (Ps. 23:4).

17

Spiritual Warfare

To the Spirit-filled believer, knowing that one has power through the name of Jesus is not a question. God's Word is clear. "All power is given unto me [Christ] in heaven and in earth" (Matt. 28:18). "Whatsoever ye shall ask the Father in my name [authority], he will give it you" (John 16:23).

The question and challenge is rather how to discern and exercise the spiritual authority we have in Christ. Therefore, the gift of discernment is among the most important to the servant of God. To discern the tactics and power (and lack of power) of the enemy is what can make even the inexperienced Christian effective in spiritual warfare.

First, Satan is the *oppressor*. While he can not possess the Christian, the devil's whole aim is to produce a "spirit of infirmity" which weakens the whole man: "Ought not this woman, being a daughter of Abraham, whom Satan hath bound, lo, these eighteen years, be loosed from this bond. . . ?" (Luke 13:16).

Satan will oppress the believer with fears, frustration and insecurity. The promises of God's Word are his defense. "If ye continue in my word. . . . ye shall know the truth, and the truth shall make you free" (John 8:31-32).

Secondly, Satan *accuses*. He is the prince of blackmailers.

In fact, he cannot condemn or judge any believer ("He that heareth my word, and believeth on him that sent me, hath everlasting life, and shall not come unto condemnation; but is passed from death unto life"—John 5:24), but he is a superb liar. The Bible describes him as "an angel of light," "a seducer," and "the accuser of the brethren."

Again, our defense against this attack is God's Word. "There is therefore now no condemnation to them which are in Christ Jesus" (Rom. 8:1). "Who is he that condemneth? It is Christ that died, yea rather, that is risen again, who is even at the right hand of God, who also maketh intercession for us" (Rom. 8:34).

Thirdly, Satan offers every possible resistance to ministry and answered prayer. When Daniel prayed earnestly for weeks for understanding, the ministering angel declared, "Fear not, Daniel: for from the first day that thou didst set thine heart to understand, and to chasten thyself before thy God, thy words were heard, and I am come for thy words. But the prince of the kingdom of Persia, withstood me one and twenty days: but, lo, Michael, one of the chief princes, came to help me. . . . Now I am come to make thee understand what shall befall thy people in the latter days" (Dan. 10:11-14, italics mine).

Frequently, the hindering power of Satan is manifested in the flesh, even in God's saints. During the time I was serving as pastor in Canada, I conducted a lot of revivals and evangelistic services. Once a pastor in Winslow, Ontario, called me to come to minister in his church and I agreed to come.

Well, before I came, he called me and said that the whole church was praying for revival but he wanted to warn me of a problem he was having. He said, "Dr. Ward, there is this dear saint in our church, but it seems like every time the Spirit begins to move, she faints into the arms of somebody near her. When this happens, it takes all the attention of the people away from the ministry at hand and quenches the Spirit. I just don't know what to do."

I agreed to pray about the situation and to still come. When I got there, I told the pastor, "I am younger than you but I believe God has given me the answer. If you will agree to let me take a calculated risk, we'll deal with this situation in God's way."

Sure enough, in our first meeting as the Spirit began to move on the hearts of the people, this lady fainted. Immediately, I asked everyone but the minister to leave the auditorium. (Jesus also often told the bystanders to leave.) This took away her audience. Then, as she lay there gasping as if in cardiac arrest, I told the assistants to open the windows.

The cold room and lack of audience had an immediate effect. She shook off her symptoms, jumped up, and snapped at me like I was the enemy, just lambasting me up one side and down the other, exhibiting the nature of her demonstrations. I simply told her, "The people of this church have come to see Jesus, and not you. They are and will give their loyalty to Jesus. If you want a part, sit down and let Him alone be exalted. Otherwise, leave." She was never a problem again.

Satan barks loud but he cannot destroy. The great preacher of City Temple in London, England, Dr. F.B. Meyer, helped me early in my ministry with what he wrote, "Don't run every time the devil tells you to!" You will learn that Satan is a *bluff.* He is a *scarecrow.*

Someone wisely said, "A wise bird sees a scarecrow as an invitation to a feast." How true! When Satan tries to throw up a block, there's obviously life and power to live around that threat.

The apostle Paul gave us all this good advice: "And having done all, to *stand*" (Eph. 6:13, italics mine). When you do not know another thing to do—*stand*. Don't run away! There *is* victory in Jesus.

18

Representing God

Each one of us who would call himself—or herself—a Christian is a representative of God. We have all heard the admonition that "we are the only Bible that many people ever read." But if we knew how true that statement really is, it would surely challenge us.

Peter understood something of the import of our words and actions when he said, "If any many speak, let him speak as the oracles of God; if any man minister, let him do it as of the ability which God giveth. . ." (1 Pet. 4:11).

As a preacher and pastor of a flock, my responsibility to represent God correctly is critical. God's judgment is reserved for His messengers who don't. "The Lord said to Eliphaz the Temanite, 'My wrath is kindled against thee, and against thy two friends: for ye have not spoken of me *the thing that is right,* as my servant Job *hath'* " (Job 42:7).

When I first pastored in Bakersfield, California, and applied for American citizenship, I unforgettably experienced the power of words expressed simply and succinctly.

Gaining my U.S. citizenship papers was for me an emotional experience on the level of the new birth and marriage. A good friend, Judge Stockton of the Superior Court, presided over the ceremony. The clerk announced the judge and the proceedings began. I geared myself to hear something like the "Gettysburg Address."

Judge Stockton, with his imposing figure and speech, asked us to rise. With the gathered crosscut of humanity, I stood waiting to be officially welcomed to the nation. The judge spoke:

> It's a great privilege to be an American. There are only two kinds of Americans—crackpots and good ones. My advice to you is: Stay with the good ones and stay away from the crackpots. Now raise your right hands!

He had taken only half a minute but he got the message across. This is what our Lord did, too. He made it "plain . . . that he may run that readeth it" (Hab. 2:2).

This experience prepared me for my many years of radio-sermon ministry as much as any other. My goal became not just to make my message interesting and relevant, but to make it clear and accurate.

During my twenty-five years as speaker on the "Revivaltime" broadcast, I was fortunate enough to have a talented editor who labored with me to make sure my messages were true and precise. I remember one incident especially where this helped avoid a potential problem.

I was preparing a message on Samson and vividly described how he killed a lion with his bare hands. Now the lion that I saw in my mind and described was our own Arizona mountain lion. But alertly, my editor pointed out, "C.M., that isn't the kind of lion that Samson faced. He met an African lion." He checked it out with librarians and I was able to give the right description over the air.

There is another reason why I have become extremely

concerned with accuracy. I've found that, just like gossip, what you say, if it is significant, is likely to be repeated.

A humorous story about other preachers giving my messages recently got back to me.

A young evangelist, apparently seeking to emulate me, took a fancy to a message I preached; it was called "Deadlines." He fastened a copy of this printed message in his Bible and preached "Deadlines" with enthusiasm and results.

Among the illustrations I used was one concerning the closing date for filing the annual income tax report. Meanwhile, the government had changed the date to later in the calendar year. Unfortunately, the young evangelist had not updated the change in the script he had fastened to his Bible.

One night, in the course of his sermon, he gave the erroneous deadline. The host pastor, sitting behind him, whispered, "It's been changed." But the young evangelist fervently repeated the former date. The pastor repeated in a much louder voice, "I said it's been changed!"

Whereupon the young evangelist turned to him and said, "It can't be; Brother Ward says so right here!"

If that is the worst inaccuracy attributed to me, I will be most grateful. The Bible alone stands infallible as truth. It alone has stood the scrutiny and verdict of history. It behooves us not only to know its truths but to line up our words and actions according to it.

In these last days, just as the Bible warns, we are being bombarded with false teachers, deceptive cults and strange doctrines. "Now the Spirit speaketh expressly, that in the latter times some shall depart from the faith, giving heed to seducing spirits, and doctrines of devils;

Speaking lies in hyprocrisy; having their conscience seared with a hot iron" (1 Tim. 4:1-2). Paul continued the description, "Having a form of godliness, but denying the power thereof. . . . Ever learning, and never able to come to the knowledge of the truth" (2 Tim. 3:5, 7). Paul commands Timothy "from such turn away," and so should we.

We see false teachers like Jim Jones, who purport to be able to work miracles, perform healings, speak in tongues and the like, thereby deceiving many. We, however, need not fear being deceived if we obey God and His Word.

The concept of *miracle* is documented in all religions. "For they cast down every man his rod, and they became serpents. . . . And the magicians of Egypt did so with their enchantments" (Exod. 7:12, 22). *But you cannot render final judgment on the basis of miracle alone.*

The raising of Lazarus did not silence or persuade the critics. "Then from that day forth they took counsel together for to put him to death" (John 11:53).

A miracle can be, and should be, a cosigner. It is always a *respectable* credential. The problem is *motive.* The automobile, which is a mechanical miracle, can be used to bring someone to Sunday school, or it can be employed by bank thieves for a getaway. Christ, who would not turn stones into bread for Satan, turned water into wine for mankind.

Authority must be the arena where validity is tested. So you go to the Word! Christ rested His case on the Word. "It is written" (Matt. 4:4).

A false prophet in 1982 is as dangerous as one in the Old Testament.

History offers a record of prophetic oracles. And the clever hedged their bets and spoke from both sides of their mouths.

Before Maxentius left Rome to meet Constantine in that famous battle on the banks of the Tiber, he consulted the "Sibylline Books." The guardians of these ancient oracles were as well-versed in the arts of this world as they were ignorant of the secrets of fate; and they returned him a very prudent answer, which might adapt itself to the event and secure their reputations, whatever should be the outcome. However, they failed to cover the fact that Maxentius was drowned in the river in his battle with Constantine.

It is always dangerous and costly to speculate—to go out on the limb.

Foreknowledge is needed to foretell.

Three tests apply.

First, it is obvious that no one can successfully foretell that which he or she does not foreknow.

Second, no one can foreknow future events to which past events furnish no key, unless aided by divine foresight. History does cast shadows. A careful collating and comparing of trends can lay the basis for rather accurate forecasting. Like causes produce like effects.

Third, the more such forecasting deals in *details*, the more impossible it is to account for it as the fruit of conjecture. A *guess* at the future, however sagacious, may not prove to be correct.

If there is a possibility for it, there is another chance against it. *Every additional factor predicted compounds this gamble and increases the odds.* The risk of failure increases.

Bible prophecy stands alone—unchallenged. God's servants accurately foretold events of a remote future— events which bear no likeness to past occurrences. They foretold with minute accuracy and precision.

Sometimes there are forty or fifty details. If one proved inaccurate, the prophecy would fail. When all are fulfilled, the testimony is that such prophecy was divinely inspired.

It is easier to counterfeit a miracle than a prophecy. Despite all the wonderful miracles the disciples saw Jesus perform and even though they heard the voice from heaven on the Mount of Transfiguration, still Peter declared, "We have also a more sure word of prophecy; whereunto ye do well that ye take heed, as unto a light that shineth in a dark place, until the day dawn, and the day star arise in your hearts" (2 Pet. 1:19).

Time and fulfillment are the measurements of prophetic truth. Fraud, falsehood or impudent presumption will be exposed if a prophetic word is not fulfilled. The Bible stands or falls by this test. Marvelous is the variety, extent and number of biblical prophecies, yet no prediction has ever failed.

Scripture invites the scrutiny and decision of history.

There is a boldness in the Bible that is unmatched by any text.

Paganism and mythology endeavored to bolster themselves by claiming to foresee the future. Their efforts are pitiful. The ends they served were often personal and selfish. *Such forecasting leaned heavily toward the box office and coffers.*

No Bible prophecy is hesitant, ambiguous or equivocal. There are no apologies. "For the prophecy came not in old time by the will of man: but holy men of God spake as they were moved by the Holy Ghost" (2 Pet. 1:21).

Speculation should be tabbed speculation.

One should be especially careful to claim inspiration.

False prophets lead others astray and are held responsible by God.

The primary idea of a prophet is "to bring to light." He or she is a person who unfolds the hidden things of God. Elisha is an example. The Holy Spirit furnishes *insight*, which is even more important than foresight. A true prophet will reject any unsound teaching even though a popular propagandist of a current fad reinforces his or her teaching with 'wonders' and 'predictions.'

The warning has been posted.

"Beloved, believe not every spirit, but try the spirits whether they are of God: because many false prophets are gone out into the world" (1 John 4:1).

"False prophets shall rise, and shall shew signs and wonders, to seduce, if it were possible, even the elect" (Mark 13:22).

False prophets feed and prosper on the gullible. The greatest protection to the flock is sound and consistent teaching in the Word of God.

As the signs of Jesus' second coming are being fulfilled all about us, scores of authors (some for profit and others sincerely) are giving us dozens of interpretations of the significance of these events in light of Bible prophecy. Rather than "taking heed to every wind of doctrine," each believer should know God's Word and allow the same Holy Spirit that inspired these prophecies to bring His understanding to light in our lives so that we may ever be ready to meet His coming.

"And when these things begin to come to pass, then look up" (Luke 21:28).

19

Breaking Routine

Something we all face and occasionally experience is monotony, the doldrums of life. The wisdom of Solomon spoke, "Where there is no vision [motivation], the people perish" (Prov. 29:18). Preachers are no exception.

Pastors must constantly guard against letting their duties become routine and ritualistic. Jesus frequently spoke against the performance of religious duties when one's heart is not in them.

I had a problem with this for a while because I thought that my feelings had to be involved to get my heart into something. But during those "sink or swim" years, I learned that I could choose to put my heart into my work and efforts. That is the key to productive and rewarding labors for Christ.

Take, for instance, leading the congregation in giving the offering. How do you keep that from becoming routine?

I mean, how many different ways can you take an offering? I found out there are at least several dozen more than most pastors have ever tried.

God loves a "cheerful giver." And making the offering time a warm, happy experience instead of a more traditional, somber, dirge-like atmosphere can be a breath of fresh air both to God and His people.

At a Bible conference, we were going to take a missionary offering for a special project in South America. When it came time in the service to collect the offering, I spoke to the people, "At this time, I want everyone who is willing to put something in the offering to stand."

A good percentage rose to their feet, but not everyone. So I pressed on, "Come on, you can all put something in, even if you have to borrow from the person next to you." Eventually everyone had taken the vow and was standing.

"Now," I continued, "I want you to promise that you'll put the money into the offering containers and not let it fall to the ground or take it back. If you aren't going to put something in and make sure it stays in the offering containers, then sit down."

Everyone remained standing.

"All right, ushers," I said, "Bring in the offering containers."

The ushers, prepared in advance, swept in from the wings pushing grocery carts, which I had prearranged to be on hand. By the time the carts passed the first row, the people realized that quarters, dimes and other coins fell through the carts and bounced to the floor. In order to keep their vows, they would have to give paper money.

On a more serious note, Reverend Clenenning of Beaumont, Texas, taught me a most inspiring means of collecting God's gifts. We were in a summer crusade and the night came when the budget for the meetings needed to be met. In that service he quietly stopped everything and announced the sum that was needed. Then, without comment, he stepped from the platform and waited for action.

He seemed so alone there all by himself, saying nothing—so isolated. I felt panic in my soul. He should be talking, urging people to rise to the occasion, doing something. But *he did nothing.*

The pressure was obvious. What would he do? What turn would the service take? Why was he risking failure? It was all so unorthodox—or was it?

Suddenly, there was a break! Someone rose and came forward and placed a bill in his hand. Quickly others found courage and came forward. It was like an altar call.

The dignity and basic honor of mankind cannot stand to abandon other human beings. There is a latent nobility which impels mankind toward rescue. When the budget was met, the audience knew they had a very real part in it and there was joy in the camp!

It was so uplifting, I decided to experiment with it myself in a mission campaign in Guyana. It not only worked, but it became a thrilling experience to have thousands of people pouring out of the grandstands in a spirit of joy to help.

God says that, "His mercies are new very morning," and I believe that every time we enter church, we should be expectant and lead our people to expect a fresh encounter with God. Little things like the appearance of the church can help to prepare the people.

Even in our musty dungeon at Woodstock, Dorothy and the other ladies added flowers, pictures and banners to spark the minds and spirits of the people. Since then, I have always tried to show evidence of God's love and goodness on the platform—whether in the form of a floral arrangement or other natural symbols.

A wonderful side benefit to that has been all the nice flowers I've been able to bring home to Dorothy.

One may wonder what can be inspiring and uplifting about a funeral? It is as certain as taxes and as final as the ticking of a clock.

But for the Christian, it is a triumphant experience—a piercing through the veil to glory. For the loved ones left behind, it is a time of hurt and sorrow, but for the departed in Christ, it is a new dimension of abundant life.

Ben Franklin wrote to George Whately, "I look upon death to be as necessary to our constitution as sleep. We shall rise refreshed in the morning."

As a pastor, my privilege was to comfort, to share the sorrow and dignity and the grief. Often the most eloquent sermon I could give in that hour was to shed a tear.

At other times, when I knew nothing of the person, it was difficult to be totally empathetic and once it even became amusing.

While I was pastor in Bakersfield, my influence and ministry grew countrywide. I was constantly being asked to minister at funerals and frequently averaged four or five a week.

On one occasion, I was asked to lead a service for a man who was not a member of the church, but listened to my weekly radio broadcast. The man was from a wealthy home and the service was held in the best funeral parlor in town.

The funeral director, Mr. Helms, at the time was president of the Morticians Association of California. He was a very proud man and a good friend. As I led the pallbearers from the chapel to the hearse, I heard the most ungodly noise. I looked back in horror to see that the coffin had broken open. It had fallen to the pavement and one entire handle was dislodged.

Apparently, the manufacturers had not bolted the

handle. They had just screwed it in, and the weight of the deceased had dislodged the handle. When the handle came out, it just dumped the coffin on the pavement, flipping the lid off.

As I looked back, one arm of the deceased was hanging out this way and one leg was over the other way. The pallbearers just stared numbly. They didn't know what to do. So I had to swing into action. I restored the hand and the leg and motioned to one of the assistant morticians to hook the lid and lift the coffin.

From then on, when I would step into chapel, I would say to Mr. Helms, "Is it bolted?" Oh, that proud man was so embarrassed.

Every pastoral function becomes a new experience in God; it is not routine. Someway, somehow, something is bound to happen to cause me to see Him, to call upon Him, to love Him and enjoy Him. May it be that way for all of us, in all of our lives: "In all thy ways acknowledge him and he shall direct thy paths" (Prov. 3:6).

Every day is a new day in God with new possibilties. Just as the priests of Israel were instructed to offer the Lord a "daily burnt offering" (Num. 29:6), we should daily offer ourselves afresh to the Lord. He will then surely keep us out of a doldrum existence.

20

Dealing With the Blues

Even the best of overcoming Christians, pastors included, have to deal with the blues now and then. Depression, discouragement and defeat are in the world and they will attack the believer. They are roadblocks to full possession of the believer's inheritance; their fruit is to rob one of the joy of living.

One of the worst of these "blues" is self-pity. Self-pity attacks people in public life perhaps more than any other seduction. When one has felt the great joy and glamour of being used of God, after the lights dim, then there is the dark trip to that solitary motel room. A great sense of emptiness attacks. Thoughts come, "Does anyone really care about me? Is it all worthwhile? Is it all a game? What happens now?" Away from caring and encouraging loved ones, these thoughts of self-doubt and criticism can surround and oppress the individual until one's joy and victory are depleted.

Self-pity is the essential problem that is revealed in most of the Canaanite kings listed in the twelfth chapter of Joshua. The book of Joshua, like Ephesians in the New Testament, is the book of battle and victory. These Canaanite kings opposed Israel's possession of the Promised Land and the book of Joshua gives us a pattern in dealing with these "blues" attacks.

Self, or the flesh, is pictured in these kings. Paul tells the Galatians, "For the flesh lusted against the Spirit, and the Spirit against the flesh: and these are contrary the one to the other: so that ye cannot do the things that ye would" (Gal. 5:17).

Self has many forms. Some of the meanings of the king's names included the following qualities of self:

Self-absorbed	Self-importance
Self-abuse	Self-improvement
Self-accusation	Self-incrimination
Self-advancement	Self-indulgence
Self-approbation	Self-love
Self-assertion	Self-made
Self-assertive	Self-pity
Self-assumption	Self-reflection
Self-centered	Self-regard
Self-condemnation	Self-respect
Self-conscious	Self-seeking
Self-esteem	

These are qualities that relate to us all. They hide deep within our souls and seek the cover of one's being. They must be sought out and destroyed. These are the kings of the country which Joshua and the children of Israel smote (Josh. 12:7).

Self-pity, each of these ego forms, is a king, a stronghold, which will withstand one's faith and victory. Each seeks to rob and steal the Christian's joy. *They must be put to death.*

When the children of Israel deferred from destroying the enemy kings and made peace with them, like they did with the Gideonites in Joshua 9, it only robbed them of purity, faith and victory. Similarly, when we are attacked with self-pity or any selfish form of self-analysis, it is certain that agreement, compromise, spiritual exercises will not help. They must be bound and defeated. "Let the high praises of God be in their mouth, and a twoedged sword in their hand; To execute vengeance upon the heathen, and punishments upon the people; To bind their kings with chains. . ." (Ps. 149:6-8).

The cure to self-centeredness is to count one's blessings. An hour's visit to any hospital will accomplish this purpose. When one sees all the limbs in traction, the burns and terminal cancer, there isn't much room for the blues and self-centeredness. I can never leave a hospital or rest home without saying, "Ward, you're a pretty fortunate fellow, so cheer up and get on with business."

This is why Jesus strongly suggested sickroom, prison and ghetto ministries. They dig out and smite self: "For I was hungered, and ye gave me no meat; I was thirsty, and ye gave me no drink: I was a stranger, and ye took me not in: naked, and ye clothed me not: sick, and in prison, and ye visited me not" (Matt. 25:42, 43).

Jesus gives the perfect antidote to self-centered living: "Give and it shall be given. . ." (Luke 6:38).

21

Music and the Sunny Side

An old proverb says, "All preachers would like to sing and all singers would like to preach." There is some truth in that statement. Many a platform has seen such a contest.

In those contests, I've never yet seen a preacher win when it comes to singing and vice versa. Many humorous incidents have happened to those who tried, however.

In one instance, we held a command service attended by all the area ministers. It was a memorial service presided over by the district superintendent. In a somber moment in the middle of the service, he decided to sing, "I Won't Have to Cross Jordan Alone."

He started out and missed the key. Soon he was struggling note by note, getting higher and higher, reaching the moment of no return. Finally, he squeaked terribly through the last few bars, coughing and sputtering. And afterwards he said, "I just received a message from the Spirit that I should read the second verse." He never did live that comment down.

Dr. Criswell of Dallas handled his miscue a little better. He had broken into a song, the southern melody, "My Lord What a Morning." But he had pitched it too high and the stars began to fall. When he knew he couldn't make it, he simply stopped and clapped, exclaiming to his congregation, "My Lord, I pitched it too high." The people enjoyed it and Dr. Criswell rejoined the human race.

I had my own share of unspectacular musical mishaps. When I was first invited to various churches to speak and evangelize, it was largely because of my musical talents on the piano. Dorothy was an even better instrumentalist, perhaps one of the finest E-flat saxophone players in the denomination.

Because God had specifically called me into the preaching ministry, after a time, we purposely downplayed our musical abilities. We chose rather to invite talented musicians to minister with us. However, I never lost my interest and appreciation of gospel music. Perhaps more than anything in the service, music has the ability to evoke the divine. The Psalmist wrote, "O sing unto the Lord a new song; for he hath done marvellous things: his right hand, and his holy arm, hath gotten him the victory" (Ps. 98:1).

Music puts us over on the sunny side of life and that is where God dwells.

The story is told of how the great coach of the Green Bay Packers, Vince Lombardi, when preparing his players for the game, would insist that his men sing in the locker room. These huge, brawny football players were exhorted to pour out melodies with every ounce of energy available. Mr. Lombardi believed that when the adrenalin was stirred and song filled the clubhouse—when it poured from his players in an uninterrupted stream— then his team was ready; they were potentially unbeatable. With music, he moved them away from doubt and apprehension to the taste of victory.

It was the same, or more so, in our great Pentecostal

song services. Just as Lombardi used music to stir his players' whole beings into action, I learned to do the same with music in our services. Soul-stirring praise pulls people to their feet, unshackles their hands, loosens their muscles and sweeps away the cobwebs of worry and doubt. Minds are freed to believe that, yes, indeed, all things are possible. There is victory in Jesus!

The great Beethoven once wrote: "Music is more than a concord of sweet sounds; it is something given from a higher world which we cannot describe, much less define; but which we have the power to invoke." Music belongs to God. He is the Author of it.

Music was one of the first arts given to man. And rightly so. No other art stirs man so deeply, so entirely—in body, mind and soul; no other sways him with such a magic spell. It is the most sensuous and spiritual of the fine arts and therein lies its power and its peril.

My interest in music was partly due to its great influence in the fledgling Pentecostal movement. The Welsh revival and Holy Spirit outpouring soon after the turn of the twentieth century largely resulted as ministers dared to loosen the "platform controlled" services with spontaneity and informal worship. Certain Americans went to Wales and returned to introduce spontaneous worship, testimony, choruses, and public confessions. This gave great impetus to the Pentecostal movement in America.

Our denomination was built on Spirit-inspired music in the service. So it shocked me when a young music director of mine asked me once, "Is God really concerned about which songs and choruses we sing in a service?" The answer is obvious, but his question made me wonder: In how many churches is the song service and worship led by the Spirit and just as Spirit-anointed as the preaching and praying?

Music under the Spirit is different from music under the law. The Bible tells us today to be "speaking to yourselves in psalms and hymns and spiritual songs" (Eph. 5:19). So in gatherings of the Body, this largely does away with paid groups dispensing music for entertainment. Under the Spirit, the music is mutual and voluntary. In the Old Testament law, there were priests and Levites, but through the gospel we are all priests.

This in no way negates the need and value of the professional Christian music groups. They will be used of God and the Holy Spirit to draw people to church and into relationship with God. Perhaps, their greatest service and opportunity is to provide music for soul-winning.

General Booth of the Salvation Army understood this great power. His rule for music was: "Let there be music and let it be soul-saving music." His bands would put step into the listeners' feet and souls.

Mr. Cyril McLellan, who worked with me for twenty-five years in the "Revivaltime" ministry, kept this in mind. He always produced a beautiful sound, a sincere and obvious message, with a "tug." One could sense in his music the "seeking" of the Savior. Mr. McLellan avoided the trap of over-arranging where the lyrics get lost in the mechanics of performance.

Soul-saving music must be felt. It is "deep calling unto deep." It shows that it is "with the heart, man believes."

So soul-saving music must evoke experience and emotion—reflecting popular styles of the day. Today that can mean anything from rock to country to jazz to classical, depending on where you are and who your audience is.

There needs to be variety in music. Paul said, "I am made all things to all men, so that I might by all means save some. And this I do for the gospel's sake, that I might be partaker thereof with you" (1 Cor. 9:22, 23).

In one of my pastorates, I had a most trying time with an associate who was serving as my music director. He was determined that one particular style of music was the most sacred and spiritual. He filled the services with it and in so doing, limited our congregation's interest and outreach.

Finally, I had to concoct a plan to deal with this stubbornness. I called him and disguised my voice. "Jim," I said, "my name is Sam Courtney and I've just moved up from Alabama. My mother has heard about your church and says that I just have to come there. I want you to know that I can really pick a mean guitar and I love country music that will really get to your people's hearts. So I am going to help you lead the music in church."

When Jim began to hem and haw and protest, I went on, "But I've already called the Reverend Ward and he says it's okay with him."

So, finally after my young associate began to get forceful and mean, I piped up proper, "This *is* your pastor—Rev. Ward!" He became a lot more tolerant of music styles after that.

Especially when it comes to music for a soul-winning invitation, it is important to reflect the culture and tradition of the area. So I will sing, "Looking For a City" in Georgia and "Living by Faith" in Oklahoma. I'll sing Wesleyan hymns in the East and western gospel songs in Texas. Some can be stirred by quartet singing and others attracted by choirs. We use different baits but remain "fishers of men."

In a recent crusade, I was preaching in Montgomery, Alabama, in a big outdoor tabernacle. After the sermon, I began the old tune, "Precious Memories, How They Linger."

The invitation lasted well over an hour. No one left the audience. It was just like a glacier that begins to move—pushing one, then another. We never left the song. It became a heartthrob and the text of the evening.

In another summer meeting in Oklahoma City, God laid a song on my heart: "Will the Circle Be Unbroken?" Suddenly, a man leaped as though he was facing assassination and gave out a piercing scream.

He was well dressed, and everything about him spoke of affluence. But it was as though a dentist had struck a nerve. The song bore right down into his soul. Perhaps he had made a vow to a dying mother and the years had numbed the promise.

This song, however, had soul-searching power like the New Testament writer declared, "dividing asunder the soul and the spirit." The man came screaming—scurrying down that aisle—as if running from the fires of hell.

Performances don't win souls, but passion will. This is the soul-winning power of music.

22

Sucker Bait

To put it bluntly, when it comes to money, many preachers (and lay Christians, too) are just plain sucker bait. They are born patsies.

They approach the subject, seemingly, with the best of intentions. That is part of the problem—they have a basic trust and love for mankind.

Traditionally, most preachers are underpaid, struggling on the lower end of the salary scale. There is always the temptation to relieve God (and His people) of financial responsibility so one can preach the gospel independently.

Perhaps more than their Protestant counterparts, Catholic priests have understood their role as gifts to their congregation. They have rightly declared that it is good, even vital, that ministers be dependent on the people.

When a minister relies upon his people for support, he is really asking them to make an investment in themselves. For how well the people support their pastor will largely determine how well he can spend his time ministering to their needs.

Fred Waring, the great band leader and Presbyterian layman, was the first person to clearly explain to me the importance of congregations making an eternal investment with their support of pastors and evangelists.

Generosity is a fruit of God's Spirit that should spread beyond the offering plate into every area of life. By tipping a minister, the individual says, "I appreciate your talent and want to help you keep doing it and doing it better." Just taking time to be with people and pray with them is a sign of generosity. And every expression of generosity we give to others will come back to us increased many-fold.

Man's basic need to give of himself to others reflects the truth that man has been created in the image of God. Even in the Garden of Eden God provided that there could be an exchange of giving between himself and man.

What could the created being of man give to his Almighty Creator God? To start, man could give his obedience. That is exactly why God put the tree of the knowledge of good and evil in the garden and forbade the eating of it—so man could experience the joy and fulfillment of giving back to God the highest gift possible, himself.

I only wish I had discovered this principle of giving earlier in life. Largely, it came to me as I saw great preachers and great singers give themselves to the people to whom they were ministering. Unlike a performance, it was total giving—love embodied in word and song.

The Master had a total sense of giving— whether it was sitting with children by the seashore or sharing His virtue to one needy woman amidst a great throng.

Jesus knew the bigness of God and how He hates littleness. Whether it was wine for the wedding, bread and fish for the hungry multitudes or transportation across Lake Galilee, Jesus was certain His heavenly Father knew the need and would provide abundantly.

How sad that many of God's servants scrimp and scrape, believing that God must be too bankrupt to help them out. And hucksters are able to play upon this attitude with amazing success.

They play upon the uncertainty of pastors' wages. Then they offer the additional opportunity to make something for retirement, or the education of the children and so on.

This temptation is what made the life of Balaam, the prophet for hire, such a tragedy. Balaam did not love unrighteousness. He loved the wages of unrighteousness. He loved God, but he loved the way sinners got paid more. This temptation faces all preachers.

Several outstanding young ministers and colleagues of mine had their ministries totally wrecked by an oil stock swindle. These men bought into a deal which had a pyramid structure, whereby they would get a percentage of what they sold to other preachers. When the hoax was discovered, they lost their pulpits and almost lost their souls. Some had dug financial holes from which it took a lifetime to recover.

I was offered a part of this, as well as a dozen or more other get-rich-fast schemes. Most of them were "limited partner" deals where I would take the financial risk while the "general partners" provide the expertise and share the "great rewards." Then there were the "invention schemes" showing fantastic drawings for some new wonder machine. In the end, you are milked and bilked, and the only return you ever get is grief.

I remember one mail order offer of an etched portrait of George Washington for just two dollars. By return mail, the buyer received a brand-new, one-dollar bill.

The experience of Dorothy and myself in that little Canadian town of Woodstock, where in the depth of the depression, we decided to trust God for His provision, has provided us a lifetime of protection from financial grief and hardship.

For there we learned not only the blessing of trusting God alone for our needs but also the blessing of giving and receiving gifts. In the form of potatoes and chickens, and five dollars a week from our star boarder, we discovered that the giver "shall in no wise lose his reward" (Matt. 10:42). And "the labourer is worthy of his hire" (Luke 10:7).

Through the giving (no matter how meager) of these Canadian people, our hearts became tied and committed in a way that could not have been otherwise. We also saw them blessed and increased through their gifts just as God promises: "Give, and it shall be given unto you; good measure, pressed down, and shaken together, and running over" (Luke 6:38).

Life's experiences have taught us that when you receive a favor—let it always be a gift outright, "only in the name of a disciple" (Matt. 10:42). Both parties are blessed and remain free. The gift, unlike a "deal," will never tie your hands.

23

Women and Marriage

This book could not be complete without some mention of women—not that even now, I know that much about them. But they are, indeed, God's most mysterious and wonderful creatures.

Personally, I am tired of hearing that women do too much in the church and should be limited in their roles of church leadership.

I have a rule of thumb. It may sound extreme, but here it is: Never hire a man unless you cannot find a woman. You will find that generally women exceed men both in productivity and loyalty. This is my experience after fifty years of public ministry.

I believe we commit a grievous error when we discourage women in our pulpits or other church positions. They were never intended to be second-class believers. Paul declares, "There is neither male nor female: for ye are all one in Christ Jesus" (Gal. 3:28).

The gospel has no sex. Should a woman have the urge to evangelize, her right, under God, is as eternal as if it were to happen to a man.

My mother was a Mennonite evangelist—and a good one. At the turn of the century, the Mennonites did just what the Salvation Army had done. They took their beautiful young women who were filled with zeal, formed them into evangelistic teams, and sent them into the hellholes of sin to rescue the perishing.

How much we miss if we do not use the talents, beauty and gifts God entrusts to us!

Again, I may sound extreme but I have found excellent success in allowing my helpmate to be my banker, budgeteer, and chancellor of the household exchequer. There will be exceptions—women who don't want to or for some reason can't handle money. But for the following reasons I believe most wives should handle the money:

1. It is degrading to a woman to have to ask or beg money from her husband. She is not a "sharecropper," but rather a full partner in the marriage contract which reads, "With all my worldly goods I thee endow."
2. By nature she is a better shopper, bargainer and buyer. She can make the available amount count for more.
3. She will be far more contented, and will spend far less on herself, when she carries the responsibility.
4. She will not be left at her wits' end should, God forbid, her husband be suddenly removed by death. She will have a practical knowledge of financial matters.

For much the same reason, Dorothy is also the furnisher, house and clothes designer, schedule maker and critic of my work. No other can be so strong and truthful and yet so loving to me with their advice.

Dorothy and I have just celebrated our fiftieth wedding anniversary and we look back over the most wonderful memories—the best years of our lives. Yet, there were thorns in our roses, too. The best of married couples, if they are honest, will admit to contentions.

The Bible speaks of the mystique of marriage, and mystique doesn't mean magic. The new philosophy that has even crept into evangelical circles proposes the wife can somehow magically and enticingly allure her husband into a beautiful, happy and fulfilling relationship.

Successful marriages take more than a veneer of sex and servility. It takes the unfolding of mutual commitment to a joined, purposeful life together for how "can two walk together, except they be agreed?" (Amos 3:3). Without the shared commitment to seek God and help each other, no amount of human effort and earthly "magic" can make a marriage work.

I remember early in our marriage there were times when I put Dorothy through great misery. We had no household furnishings, no car, no nice clothes for her. Here she was, hundreds and hundreds of miles away from home and without family or friends. With all this, on rare occasions, she would get discouraged.

In times like this, I first tried to talk her out of her discouragement. That just made us both miserable and more irritable. So finally, I learned to say, "Honey, evidently you're unhappy. Why don't you just go into the bedroom and lock me out? I'll answer the phone and the door. Take as much time as you wish and tell Jesus about your problem. Tell Him that you really don't have the clothes that you'd like to have. Tell Him that you feel you need an automobile and you're tired of living on this street. He may agree with you and if He does, I work for Him and He'll let me know."

In the marriage, a man must hold the reins of spiritual

129

leadership if he is to keep the respect of his wife. But he must also demonstrate undying devotion to his wife. The story of Dr. Johnathan Goforth, the great Presbyterian missionary to China, taught me a great lesson about this.

Buried in the hinterlands of backward China during this ministry, Mrs. Goforth grew restless and left her godly husband. He did not follow but was at the station to meet the train which came every other week. Upon returning, Mrs. Goforth asked as she ran into her husband's arms, "But how did you know I would be on that train?"

He simply replied, "Because you work for the same Man I do." We love because He first loved us.

In counseling with hundreds of married couples over the years, I discovered that nearly all marriages fall into one of nine possible arrangements:

1. *Husband is the leader—but he is detached.* He is good but he is a robot. The routine has become *mechanical.* He withdraws rather than confronts. She has learned to *hold in* and *hold back.* She accepts. She has security without pleasure. Her personal sacrifice is for the welfare of the children.

   Much of this is reflected in the Jacob-Leah arrangement (see Gen. 29-31).

2. *Husband is the leader—but he is aggressive and combative.* He is loud and *abusive.* He is a despicable bully. He is grouchy and boasts that he "wears the pants" in the family.

   She sandpapers this image by nagging. She has learned ways to sidestep his 'would-be' authority. She knows that, inwardly, he is not as sure of himself as he pretends to be, outwardly.

   A good Bible study of this subject is the Nabal-Abigail contract (1 Sam. 25).

3. *Husband is the leader—but he is a perpetual heckler. There's noise, but never violence.* There are lots of put-downs on both sides which friends never take seriously. *Jibes* seem to be a way of life with this marriage.

   He doesn't want his wife to work. He would rather not be involved with her family. He likes to think he is successful. She is not convinced.

   David treated Michal like this (see 1 Sam. 18, 19; 2 Sam. 3, 6).

4. *Husband is the leader—he is a charmer with a magnetic personality.* He is a good *family man.* He tries always to make the home a place of fun. He believes laughter is the cure for most wrinkles in marriage. Her life is given to him. She has emancipated herself from all other ties. Neither gets along very well with her mother.

   Many of these elements enter the relationship between Boaz and Ruth (Ruth 2-4).

5. *Husband is the leader—he is cooperative.* This is an enviable working arrangement. There is mutual respect. This couple desires little company other than themselves.

   She is very close to her mother, who has burdened her with a load of "shoulds" about the way a wife *should* behave. She tends toward self-righteousness and can be overly 'religious.' She accepts her husband's conclusions as *ex-cathedra.*

   Much of this is seen in the ties between Isaac and Rebecca (Gen. 22-27).

6. *Wife is the leader—she has a take-charge attitude.* The husband is always the *minor* in the organization.

She rules the roost. She is shrill and demanding and *resourceful*. The public tags him as henpecked. She uses the 'cold shoulder' and the 'hot tongue' to get her own way.

He endures it because he has been *conditioned*.

Examine the Ahab-Jezebel coupling (1 Kings 16-21).

7. *Wife is the leader—by default.* He goes his own way with as little fuss as possible. It's a *pallid* marriage. Both are insecure.

    He will not get ahead. She fears for the economy of the marriage. He is sort of a namby-pamby, mother's boy who has never quite reached manhood.

    There is a lot of this in the marriage of Zebedee (Matt. 20:20; 27:56).

8. *Wife is the leader—in a congenial situation.* This is a happy couple who are *low-key*. They avoid strain. They do not make excessive demands upon each other. He is not *competitive*. He takes pride in her accomplishments.

    Much of this happy element is seen in the home of Elizabeth and Zacharias (Luke 1).

9. *Shared leadership—the ideal.* He loves his work and takes pride in it. She is the 'lady' of the household. They exchange views and input. They avoid *superlatives*. Their target is a smooth-running relationship. They enjoy what others believe is boring. Moses and Zipporah must have known much of this peace (Exod. 2-4).

    Another beautiful picture of marriage love is seen in Aquila and Priscilla's relationship (Acts 18; Rom. 16:3; 1 Cor. 16:19; 2 Tim. 4:19).

Today, I still know far from everything about marriage and the "feminine mystique" but I know that God knows all about it. He loves all our helpmates. He made them to fulfill our lives—and He causes us to be united in joy as one.

The courtship, the intrigue, the attraction never ceases. This is the secret to longevity—the joy of married life. "Two are better than one."

24

Fullness of Joy

Life as a pastor and radio preacher has been great! Even Bible school was fantastic!

No, I didn't learn everything in Bible school. I still haven't stopped learning. If the eyes of our hearts are open to the Almighty God, we'll never stop learning. Every day is a new thrill, a new adventure into the depths of His love.

God has woven His lovingkindness into all His creation and His people. And His people are the best. As I said before, I believe God is crazy about people and so am I.

One beautiful verse from David has so blessed me all these years that I must share it with you. The promise of God declares, "Thou wilt shew me the path of life: in thy presence is fulness of joy; at thy right hand there are pleasures forevermore" (Ps. 16:11).

This tells me that God will guide me through the storms, the joys, the temptations, the trials and the challenges of life—and all the while, keep me on the sunny side of life.

Yes, there have been times when I've messed up and failed badly. But even they have had their purpose in God's wonderful plan. So there has been no need for regrets and I believe *regret* is the heaviest load a human being can carry.

Regret speaks of that which is lost and can't be regained—not so, for the Christian, for the believer. No matter what our age, our station, what we've been, what we are, what we are not, God promises to show us and lead us down the path of life—eternally.

In His constant presence, I find fullness of joy—not fear of failure, not condemnation, not hassles and laborious struggle, not harsh rules and rituals—but deep and rich joy. If heaven were as dull and harsh as many preachers make it seem to be on Sunday mornings, I think I'd rather take a rain check. But, no, this is not the delightful heavenly Father I know. My God says, "It is good!" This is my inheritance (and yours, too) as His child.

Finally, I see that at God's right hand, which is everywhere, there are pleasures abundant and eternal. Yes, many are deeply hidden. But seeking them out is one of the great joys and adventures of life. Our God is so great and rich and loving, it will take us all eternity to discover Him in all His wonder. When we get to heaven we will continually eat of the tree of life and partake of that hidden manna that perfectly satisfies. God has promised us not only a mansion, but a new name—we will be redeemed from all darkness, sin and death.

Life is wonderful now and it is just a foretaste of the glory we'll personally share with Jesus through all the ages of eternity. Yes, life is one great, exciting learning experience for all of us!